A mom's world tends to be ruled by her family's demands, her day planner, meal preparations, e-mail, phone calls, and all other last minute emergencies. When you add a home-based business to the mix, it's hard to balance it all. Kendra Smiley's helpful new book, *High-Wire Mom*, could permanently change your life for the better. In addition to practical advice with a humorous twist, she helps women answer the question: "What's really important?" The book includes fifty time management tips, "quick fix" recipes, and inspiration for the soul that will assist you in outlining a personal master plan that works.

> Carol Kent, president
> Speak Up Speaker Services
> National speaker and author

With her own delightful humor, Kendra challenges us to give up good for better, and better for best. Her watercolor picture of top priorities influencing each below is classic. It is an inviting read.

> J. Otis and Gail Ledbetter
> Cofounders, Heritage Builders Association

I wish I had had Kendra's book early in my own home-based business. It would have saved me from making some of the most common mistakes of trying to balance too many opportunities and not enough time. Kendra has successfully walked the tightrope of being a wife and mother and having a home-based business. She lives what she says. I've been in her home and eaten her delicious Tater Tot Breakfast Casserole. If you want to have a home-based business that doesn't shortchange your family or compromise your relationship with God, listen to her wise advise. Her three boys (now young men), and her husband love God, love each other, and love her. That says it all.

> Leslie Vernick,
> Christian counselor, popular speaker, and author

Kendra Smiley is the mom every kid (and grown-up kid!) wishes they had. She's also one of the most down-to-earth, generous, hilarious women I know. In *High-Wire Mom,* Kendra answers my burning question: "How does a mother have an outgoing life of her own, and still create a home so full of joy that her husband and kids love and adore her?" Kendra has somehow managed to do this. I've been in her home, I met her family. She's truly amazing. And she's the Real Deal.

Inquiring moms will want to read . . .

Becky Freeman
Best-selling author and national speaker

To: Ray Ann

Balancing
Your Family
and a
Business
@ Home

KENDRA
SMILEY

HIGH
WIRE
MOM

MOODY PRESS
CHICAGO

*Kendra
Smiley
(John 8:32)*

To the memory of my good friend
and Home-Based-Business Mom mentor,
Shirley Dahlquist

CONTENTS

Foreword by Cheri Fuller   9

Acknowledgments   11

Introduction: The Big Top   13

PART ONE:
PUTTING FIRST THINGS FIRST

1. Establishing Your Priorities: Your **Time Investment**   21
2. My First Priority: The Lord   29
3. My Second Priority: My Husband   35
4. My Third Priority: My Children   39
5. My Fourth Priority: My Work   47
6. My Fifth Priority: Other Good Things   53

PART TWO:
KNOWING WHAT YOU'RE DOING AND WHY

7. Establishing Your "Jobs" Description: 61
   Your **Time Commitment**

Defining Your Home-based Business
8. Gaining Personal Fulfillment   63
9. Earning Supplemental Income   67
10. Being the Breadwinner   73
11. The Need for Good Communication   77

Describing Your Home-based Responsibilities
12. Your Key Responsibility: Homemaking   87
13. Your Recurring Responsibility: Housekeeping   99
14. The Motivation for Your Responsibility: Family   109

Delighting in Your Home-based Faith
15. Taking Time for a Relationship with Your Savior   119

PART THREE:
USING YOUR TIME WISELY

16. Establishing Balance in Your Home and Business: 129
    Your **Time Management**
17. The Master Plan of Time Management   133
18. 50 Nifty Time Management Hints   151
19. Recipes That Are *Really* Easy   161
    . . . but Make You Look Good!

Conclusion: Back to the Big Top   173
Appendix: Books on My Shelf   175
That You Might Want on Yours

FOREWORD

Reading Kendra Smiley's book *High-Wire Mom* brought back so many memories of when I left a full-time teaching position to embark on the adventure of a home-based business almost twenty years ago. Instead of heading for the classroom each morning and staying up late grading English papers, I put a load of laundry in and went straight to my computer after the kids left for school. Then at 3:30 I shut the door to the office and was fully "Mom." Yes, I found I needed to drop tennis league and a daytime Bible study to focus on my goals as a writer, speaker, and consultant. But I found the sacrifices were more than worth it for the benefits.

My stress level decreased and I had more energy for my children (much needed for all kids, but especially when they reach the teen years!). There also was more of me left at the end of the day to pour into their emotional tanks. It wasn't that I didn't work—quite the contrary. I put lots of effort into going for my goals. But the time flexibility, the opportunity to attend their after-school games, have a Coke with Alison, throw the ball with Chris before dinner, and be there when they were home sick, was invaluable. In fact, those two words—"being there"—sums up perhaps the greatest benefit of being a home-business mom. You can *be there* for your kids at every stage.

Looking back now since Justin, Chris, and Alison are all three grown and married, I wouldn't trade my years as a home-business mom. Not for a big retirement fund, a title, monetary gain, or anything else. I had the best of both worlds—the blessing of being a mother who was actively involved in the lives of my children and the opportunity to have a career, a creative outlet, and a way to make income all at the same time.

From not only my own experience, but that of many women I've interviewed through the years—the home-based publicist, the graphic artist, the cross-stitch kit designer, the adoption agency director, the Creative Memories consultant, to name a few—I firmly believe that working from home offers women the best opportunity to keep their priorities straight, make income, and engage in a business they love, all the while giving their kids and husbands the love and care they need and honoring God with their lives. And since I wrote my book *Home Business Happiness* in 1995, the technology has advanced even more, making home-based businesses even more workable and efficient.

There are many challenges and obstacles to running a home-based business, but the advice Kendra offers in *High-Wire Mom* will give you the inspiration you need to fire your efforts and the practical help to balance household, business, and mothering so you won't burn out after the first or second year. Kendra's "Master Plan" time management method is a great way to get organized and make the most of your time—I wish I'd had it when I first started.

Kendra writes with a lively humor and lots of wisdom, so you'll enjoy reading the pages ahead. Her book is a must-read for those who want to walk the high wire as a home-business mom!

—Cheri Fuller

ACKNOWLEDGMENTS

The acknowledgments for this book travel back through the ages to when I first became a home-based-business mom more than twenty years ago. By naming specific people I run a tremendous risk of missing someone very significant. So I have opted not to take that risk. You know who you are. You taught me and encouraged me and laughed with me and cried with me as I learned about being a home-based-business mom. Thanks for the memories and the mentoring.

Thanks to the home-based-business moms (and CEOs of home-based businesses) who, through the years, have allowed me to teach them and their cohorts the concepts in this book. You were my guinea pigs as I defined and refined the notions, instructions, motivation, and inspiration that appear in this book. You also know who you are.

A person can't be a home-based-business mom without kids. Thank you, Matthew, Aaron, and Jonathan, for sending me out the door with a smile and with another funny story to tell. Thanks for seeing value in the work I did as a home-based-business mom. Thanks for being proud of your mom.

And I cannot write an acknowledgment without highlighting the first and second most important people in my life . . . Jesus and John. I do not deserve the love of either, but I am truly appreciative for the love of both!

INTRODUCTION:
THE BIG TOP

The house lights dim as the spotlights weave and circle, illuminating the center ring. A wire is stretched high in the air between two very tall stands. The booming voice of the ringmaster sounds from the speakers.

"Ladies and gentlemen, please give your attention to the center ring. In just a moment you will witness an amazing feat. Mom, a woman near and dear to all of our hearts, will climb up this ladder with agility and poise and will position herself to walk the high wire to the opposite stand. On that stand she has placed her goals. Can you see them? They include loving and serving God, her husband, and her children and successfully running a home-based business.

"If she can keep her balance on the high wire and actually reach those goals, she will truly be worthy of our applause. Remember, Mom is balancing her commitment to not just one, not just two, but three young children, her husband, their household, her church responsibilities, *and* a home-based business.

"Can she do it? Can she reach the goals on the far stand? Will she need to discard some of her commitments as she traverses the wire? We all know that she cannot sacrifice the most important things or she will never reach her goals. What an incredible feat of daring! Watch closely. It's THE HOME-BASED-BUSINESS MOM!"

Could the home-based-business mom really be featured in the center ring of the Big Top? Is the feat she plans to attempt really amazing enough to dazzle onlookers? Or perhaps the question should be—*Can* a mother with a home-based business actually achieve those goals? Can she have success as someone who honors God and is a wife and parent *and* the owner of a home-based business?

THE DO-IT-ALL GAL

Are you familiar with the Proverbs 31 woman? Some of you probably are, and some of you may not be. In fact, many of you know the woman I'm referring to, and you really aren't very fond of her. I can understand why. She has sort of a bad reputation among women because, well, actually, because she had such a good reputation.

Do you follow me? Her goals were similar to the home-based-business mom. Let's take a look at *her* high-wire act. "A wife of noble character who can find? She is worth far more than rubies. Her husband has full confidence in her and lacks nothing of value. She brings him good, not harm, all the days of her life" (Proverbs 31:10–12).

It appears she's doing a good job of walking that high wire of loving and serving her husband. She's also got a handle on loving her kids. "Her children arise and call her blessed; her husband also, and he praises her" (Proverbs 31:28).

Everyone in that household would say she has met the goals of loving and serving her husband and children. And, according to her hubby, her commitment to the Lord is not shabby either. He comments regarding her that "a woman who fears the Lord is to be praised" (Proverbs 31:30b).

And this amazing Proverbs 31 woman also seems to have a successful home-based business.

She selects wool and flax and works with eager hands. She is like the merchant ships, bringing her food from afar. She gets up while it is still dark; she provides food for her family and portions for her servant girls. She considers a field and buys it; out of her earnings she plants a vineyard. She sets about her work vigorously; her arms are strong for her tasks. She sees that her trading is profitable, and her lamp does not go out at night. (Proverbs 31:13–18)

This woman seems to have walked the high wire and reached her goals. It appears that she does it all! At least we *assume* she does it all, and that's what is so annoying about her. But does she? Can anyone walk the high wire to her goals and do it all? What is the definition of "all"? Look again at Proverbs 31:15 where it refers to "her servant girls." My guess is that her staff gave a big contribution to the "all" that was accomplished.

Can you be successful as a wife and mother, have a home-based business, and honor God with your life? Yes. But it is not a simple matter. Just as the professional high-wire performer spends hours and hours practicing her art and the Proverbs 31 woman's "lamp does not go out at night" (verse 18b), a home-based-business mom must exhibit dedication and focus.

The high-wire star must give up certain things that might impede her performance or negatively influence her success . . . things like banana splits after eight P.M. (or maybe even *before* eight). The Proverbs 31 woman must release some responsibilities to others. And Mom will discover that she, too, must sacrifice some things. She will have to determine the things that do not aid her in reaching her goals and reject those. They are not necessary. In fact, at times they can actually be a detriment. The home-based-business mom must learn when to say yes to opportunities and commitments and when to say no. Mom cannot do it all and reach her goals. As pointed out in a recent Sunday cartoon, the woman in the television commercial who does it all "only has to sustain it for thirty seconds."

I'M A HOME-BASED-BUSINESS MOM

By training (read: money invested), I am a teacher. I have bachelor's and master's degrees in education. Teaching school was always a pleasure for me. I enjoyed almost every aspect of the job. After discovering, however, that my husband and I were expecting our first child, the assignment of being a mom took precedence. I put my teaching career on hold, and I became an at-home mom. That was in the fall of 1978. Matthew was born in October, and I began my new career pursuit—motherhood.

By staying home with Matthew, I learned that I would now have time to give attention to certain things I had chosen to ignore while teaching school and coaching girls' athletics. Now, I discovered, I had ample time and opportunity to actually dust. This realization was not necessarily comforting, for I had no desire to dust. In truth, I suddenly realized the fact that my busyness away from home *before* Matthew was born (i.e., teaching school, coaching, choir, Sunday school teaching, etc.) had provided a wonderful explanation for my lack of enthusiasm for things like dusting. And now, alas, the excuse had vanished.

With tongue in cheek, I have been known to explain that my initial interest in starting a home-based business stemmed from my need for a *new* legitimate reason not to dust. That is at least partially true.

Actually, there were other factors too. I am a "people person." Some of you can empathize with a people person who has only one very little person around her for the great majority of the day. Matthew was delightful, but he was unable to meet my need for conversation or adult interaction. A home-based business provided a wonderful, legitimate resource for people—one of my favorite things. A home-based business appealed to me because it met that need in my life.

Add to those two motivators the fact that, before our first child was born, both my husband and I were teaching school. Teachers' salaries are typically based on formal education and experience. Because I have my master's degree and John has his bachelor's, my "retirement" from teaching meant that our family took a pay cut of more than 50 percent. Because of that monetary adjustment, I learned some interesting skills, like the art of watering down the ketchup and the inventiveness of using laundry detergent on the dishes when necessary. The idea of a home-based business making a monetary contribution to the family was appealing (even if it only provided an occasional fast-food lunch or a movie).

In addition to these pluses, perhaps the most important factor that I discovered as I researched home-based businesses was the realization that I would not have to leave my home according to someone else's schedule. If my husband, John, was home in the evening, I could use that time for business. I was not forced to leave my child and our home. The schedule was my decision.

All of the selling points you hear when it comes to home-based businesses appealed to me. I could set my own hours. I could be my own boss. I could earn extra income. I could interact with adults. And, of course, the seldom espoused, much appreciated perk—I could legitimately ignore the dusting!

So Matthew arrived in October of 1978 and I officially became a home-based-business mom in January of 1980. Since that time, two more sons have been added to the family (Aaron in 1981 and Jonathan in 1985), and my home-based business has evolved from a direct-selling business to professional speaking and writing. And along the way, I have learned valuable lessons. Lessons about the importance of establishing priorities and the application of those priorities in my life. Lessons about honest evaluation. Lessons about motherhood (and wifehood). Lessons about time management. Lessons about getting rid of some of my responsibilities and not trying to do it all. And lessons about the Lord.

If you are contemplating the duplication of the high-wire act of becoming a home-based-business mom, or if you have already started walking that tightrope, this book is for you. You will not discover the perfect filing system or how to evaluate a franchise agreement. You won't get tax tips or information on how to dress for success. Instead, we'll examine the valuable insights in God's Word and illustrate His wisdom with lessons I've learned from twenty-plus years as a mom and the owner of a home-based business. Join me in the pages of this book as I tell some lessons I have learned. My desire is to equip, encourage, and motivate all you moms who hear the call to have a home-based business (and, if you're like me, to avoid the dusting).

PART ONE:

PUTTING FIRST THINGS FIRST

*"Creating a list of priorities is not enough!
I must paint a picture."*

ESTABLISHING YOUR PRIORITIES:
YOUR TIME INVESTMENT

"Establish your priorities" was the instruction—a directive I had received many times before. I did not have to be convinced that the establishment of priorities was important. I had already been sold on that idea. In fact, several things had occurred to convince me of the importance of honestly evaluating my priorities and determining where I wanted to invest my time. What *was* truly important to me?

ENJOY THOSE BOYS

As I began my speaking career, I was eager to speak for any group or organization that called. I looked at that time in my professional life as an experience similar to student teaching. Student teaching, or practice teaching, usually occurs in a future teacher's last year in college. The teacher trainee pays tuition to the university and is assigned to a school and a cooperating teacher in order to practice his or her skills. In essence, the student teacher is paying to be allowed to practice.

With beginning speaking it was *a little* better . . . even though I didn't receive much compensation, at least I didn't have to pay! While on those "student speaking" assignments, I attended a lot of monthly meetings for ladies' groups. Next I graduated to mother-daughter banquets . . . many, many mother-daughter banquets. And it was at those banquets that I heard a common note. Invariably I would tell funny (and true) stories about my sons, and invariably a grandma-lady would speak to me after the program, saying something like, "Honey, enjoy those boys. They'll be gone before you know it!" And it always seemed that the unspoken finish to that sentence was "because, you see, I didn't, and now they are gone."

This didn't just happen once, but time and time again. That was my first persuader to establish my priorities.

THE OLDLY-WED GAME

When the time came to celebrate my in-laws' fortieth anniversary, the kids and kids-in-law organized a party. As a part of the entertainment on that special day, we played the Oldly-Wed Game. The contestants included the honored duo and three other couples who qualified as oldly-weds. We separated each husband and wife, and the questioning began. The goal of each couple was to match their answers and score.

To this day, the only question and answer I can remember is the following: To the husband—What is your wife's favorite saying? "Oh, this one is easy," said one particular contestant. "My wife's favorite saying is 'Hurry up!'"

Do I need to tell you that this answer did *not* match his wife's? Her answer was something sweet and mushy, and she was not thrilled by the answer her husband had given.

"Hurry up!" Hmmmmmmm, how would *my* husband answer the question "What is your wife's favorite saying?" How would my children? What would they put as an epitaph on my tombstone? "Here lies Mom. We'll always remember her saying, 'Hurry up!'" Or worse yet, "I'm too busy!" Yikes! It dawned on me that day that I had better sow the seeds now for what I hoped would grow in the future when it was time for *us* to play the Oldly-Wed Game. What *were* my priorities?

GONE FISHING

And then came the final impetus—the one I needed to get serious about evaluating what was truly important to me and establishing my priorities. I am the baby in my family. I have an older sister (ten years my senior) and an older brother (twelve years my senior). The long period of time between numbers one and two and me made for many interesting dynamics, most of which I have come to genuinely appreciate.

My sister went to college when I was eight years old, and within the first year away she met the man of her dreams. When she was twenty, her beau was getting pretty serious about courting her, and this young man wisely included me on many occasions. When Christmas rolled around, he brought a present for her and one for me too. (Smart man, right? I guess he figured he was securing my vote.)

And I loved him! When I was twelve, they were married. My brother-in-law, Tom, continued to be one of my favorite people for years and years. He also became my dentist after my father (and original dentist) died.

One day, more than a decade ago, Tom and I were talking. He was explaining to me that he was having difficulty making extractions. He told me that the task involves some degree of strength, and that he was not feeling as strong as usual. After that conversation and after some unsuccessful attempts to regain his strength, he finally visited his physician.

The doctor suspected something serious and scheduled tests. Within days, my brother-in-law was diagnosed with a brain tumor. A short time after that, he underwent surgery. The prognosis following the surgery was bleak. The surgeon had not been able to remove the entire tumor. It was cancerous, and the doctors anticipated that Tom would not regain enough strength for chemotherapy or radiation.

The next few weeks were difficult for my sister, her children, and everyone who loved Tom. I tried to visit with him every other day. Actually, "visiting" is a not an accurate word. Communication was very difficult. So typically, on each visit, I did a monologue, which he seemed to enjoy. When he did speak, I was quick to listen, because the verbal exchanges were few and far between.

One day as I sat with him, patted him, and generally encouraged him, Tom said something I hope I never forget. "Sister," he said with an audible sigh, "I should have gone fishing more."

That was it. "I should have gone fishing more." That statement hit me right between the eyes, and I vowed that to the best of my ability I would live each and every day with intent and purpose. I knew I needed to get a grasp on what was important to me and to see to it that I had as few regrets as possible. I wanted to be as sure as I could that at forty-five (Tom's age when he died) or fifty-five or sixty-five or seventy-five or eighty-five or one hundred and five, that I had fished and hugged and read and done all the important things on my list with all the important people on my list. I wanted to invest my time wisely.

SO . . .

I was more convinced than ever that the establishment of priorities was important. I quickly listed my top five—the rankings I had determined long ago.

1. The Lord
2. My husband, John
3. My three sons
4. My work
5. Other good things

There, that's done. I had (for the umpteenth time) made my list of priorities. And as certain as I was that this was an accurate list of the important things in my life, I was just as sure that I would have difficulty making application of the list to my life. After all, how would this list have a practical application? How could a list influence my life?

RANKING AND TIME ALLOTMENT

Let's see . . . God is number one. Does a number one position indicate that He deserves or requires the majority of my time? Perhaps God should get eight of the twenty-four hours in a day. Then maybe my husband, John (number two on the list), should receive seven hours. Now let's see, 8 + 7 = 15 and 24 – 15 = 9. OK. I still have nine hours to allot. If the boys get four (not too practical at many of the child-rearing stages when they need or demand more hours) that would be approximately one hour and twenty minutes per child. I still have five hours remaining. Undoubtedly, I should divide it by giving three hours to work and two hours to "other good things."

Wait! It just occurred that I have failed to consider, among other things, the eight hours of sleep I require each night! If my Bible is on my nightstand, perhaps I can capitalize on a few of those sleeping hours—you know, count them in my God tally. Or, maybe because John and I are sawing logs side by side, the sleeping hours can go toward his seven hours.

Ridiculous? Yes! But questions and thoughts just like these surfaced each time I created my list of priorities. As persuaded as I was that the concept of establishing a list of priorities was a good one, I was always stymied by the application of the list to my life. Until . . .

WATERCOLOR PAINTING

One day I was involved in one of the many mundane tasks of housekeeping—cleaning the tub, as I recall—and I was amusing myself by trying to solve the "Puzzle of the Priorities" that had plagued me for years. As I pondered the elusive application of my list to my life, I had an idea. This idea was so much bigger than the ones I typically have that I wondered if perhaps it was an idea from God.

Over the years, my lists of priorities had always been done with pen or pencil and paper . . . numbering from 1 to 5. The new idea that I had was based on the use of an entirely different medium—watercolors.

What if I *painted* my priorities rather than writing them with pen or pencil? What if I chose watercolor paper and paints *and* placed the pad of paper upright instead of on a flat surface?

Some of you with experience in watercolor painting are shaking your heads in warning. "That won't work, Kendra," you're saying. "The colors will run if the paper is not flat. The colors at the top of your painting will drip all the way to the bottom of the page."

Precisely. Can you see the picture? God is painted at the top of the paper, and the watery color that has sketched His name is pulled by gravity toward the bottom of the page. The color chosen to write John's name, my number two priority, is influenced or colored by the dripping paint of my number one priority. And, of course, both colors then join together to continue the march to the bottom of the page.

My sons are painted into the number three spot with a different color and are quickly colored by both God and their dad as they join the journey down the page. The color of priority number four, my work, is altered by all three preceding colors and, of course, number five—other good things—is influenced by every other color/priority on the list.

The picture I saw in my imagination that morning may not have been pretty by artistic standards, but it was beautiful to me. Finally I had an application I could understand. My number one priority, God, did not stand alone, but instead colored and influenced each of my other priorities. Decisions made about my children were colored by the priorities of both God and my husband, John. Work opportunities and responsibilities (priority number four) were colored and considered in light of the Lord, my husband, and my children. And finally, all those "other good things" that can crowd our lives were weighed and evaluated by the priorities above on the list . . . the things I had already deemed the better and the best.

With this idea in mind, I want to encourage you to paint your priorities *and* to determine where you want to invest your time.

Remember to allow the first priority in your life to color each thing on your list . . . to allow the preceding priorities to influence those beneath them.

But first, let's walk through my list of priorities with more explanation as to how each item on the list obtained its ranking. The next few chapters will take you along the path I traveled to establish my list. Ultimately, the establishment of your list and the all-important watercolor painting of that list will be up to you. Perhaps the path I traveled will be a guide.

First things first. We'll begin with my number one priority, the Lord.

2

MY FIRST PRIORITY:
THE LORD

God is first on my list. Actually, I'm just reflecting an idea started years ago. When God gave Moses the Ten Commandments, the number one position was filled with these words: "I am the LORD your God, who brought you out of Egypt, out of the land of slavery. You shall have no other gods before me" (Exodus 20:2–3).

God is adamant about occupying the first spot. In fact, in both the Old and New Testaments, He is described as "a consuming fire, a jealous God" (Deuteronomy 4:24; Hebrews 12:29). I'd say that is pretty clear, yet it is still tough for me to always remember who is in first place.

More than once I've thought that God could have made it a little easier for me. Let's say, for example, that my assigning God to the number one spot on my list manifested itself by my choice to spend time each morning in His Word and in prayer. And, just for

HIGH-WIRE MOM

the sake of argument, let's say that I missed a day. Now *what if*, as I left the house on that forgetful day, I noticed God waiting for me on the front porch. (I realize this is bad theology, but stay with me.) He knows I've failed to spend time with Him so far that day, and so, as a gentle reminder, He shakes His head in disappointment and sends me back into the house.

Now who in the world would want God to be disappointed? The open manifestation of that disappointment would be enough to convince me to keep my priorities in order. And, truly, God *is* disappointed when we fail to meet Him in His Word and in prayer, but He does not force us to go "back into the house" until we get it right. Wouldn't that be easier? Maybe it would, but it would not be in God's nature, for He gives us the freedom to choose to love Him and serve Him and obey Him and need Him. We choose to have no other gods before Him.

SOMETHING FISHY

God gives us the freedom to choose, but in some cases in Scripture God was a little more punitive when it came to disobedience. Take Jonah, for example. God told Jonah what to do. God said, "Go to the great city of Nineveh and preach against it, because its wickedness has come up before me" (Jonah 1:2).

It is recorded that Jonah decided *not* to do what God instructed. In fact, he headed for Tarshish. "But Jonah ran away from the LORD and headed for Tarshish. He went down to Joppa, where he found a ship bound for that port. After paying the fare, he went aboard and sailed for Tarshish to flee from the LORD" (Jonah 1:3).

This particular case of disobedience did not sit well with the Lord. God stirred up the wind and the sea, and the ship carrying Jonah away from Nineveh was in serious trouble. Finally, after the sailors had dumped most of the supplies, Jonah convinced the others that he was the cause of the storm. When he was confronted by the ship's crew, Jonah was quick to suggest a solution. "'Pick me up and throw me into the sea,' he replied, 'and it will become calm. I know that it is my fault that this great storm has come upon you'" (Jonah 1:12).

30

Although the crew seemed to feel guilty about the maneuver, the men finally did pick Jonah up and throw him into the sea. Immediately it became calm.

This was good news for the mariners, but not necessarily for Jonah. He was to spend the next three days (and three nights) in the belly of a great fish. Jonah knew why he was there, and as he recognized the error of his ways, he cried out to God, "and the LORD commanded the fish, and it vomited Jonah onto dry land" (Jonah 2:10). And God gave Jonah a second chance. He told him, "Go to the great city of Nineveh and proclaim to it the message I give you" (3:2). This time Jonah obeyed.

Can you see the beauty of this plan? Jonah did not repeat his mistake of disobedience. Can you imagine if this divine intervention occurred in our lives?

GOD: *Kendra, go into the house and read My Word and pray.*

KENDRA: *Is the belly of a great fish my only other option?*

GOD: *Well . . .*

KENDRA: *OK. I'll go!*

Pretty effective, but not God's plan for me or for you. We must choose obedience when the consequences of disobedience are not necessarily so obvious. We must choose to honor God as our number one priority because of our love for Him.

A RELATIONSHIP

God is in the number one spot on my list. Did you notice that I did not say going to church is in first place? Don't get me wrong; I like going to church and I'm aware that God recommends it too. "Let us not give up meeting together, as some are in the habit of doing" (Hebrews 10:25). But going to church, and meeting together, is not all there is to worshiping God. I can have a relationship with individuals in a church, but, as important as those individuals may be to me, Jesus is number one.

My relationship with the Lord is exactly that—a relationship. It is amazing to contemplate (yet absolutely true) that God, the Creator of the universe, and His Son, Jesus Christ, desire to have a relationship with me. And They want one with you too . . . a personal, passionate relationship. Christ said, "Whoever does God's will is my brother and sister and mother" (Mark 3:35). As we love and obey God and do His will, we are in relationship with the Son and the Father.

"Because you are sons, God sent the Spirit of his Son into our hearts, the Spirit who calls out, 'Abba, Father'" (Galatians 4:6).

"How great is the love the Father has lavished on us, that we should be called children of God!" (1 John 3:1).

BY POPULAR DEMAND

So, is the Lord in the top spot just because He demands it? No, although that is a good enough reason. "The fear of the LORD is the beginning of wisdom; all who follow his precepts have good understanding. To him belongs eternal praise" (Psalm 111:10).

God occupies the first position not only because He lovingly demands it, but because He is deserving of it. Read some of His attributes, some of the promises regarding the Lord:

But you are a shield around me, O LORD; you bestow glory on me and lift up my head. To the LORD I cry aloud, and he answers me from his holy hill. I lie down and sleep; I wake again, because the LORD sustains me. (Psalm 3:3–5)

We wait in hope for the LORD; he is our help and our shield. (Psalm 33:20)

The LORD will keep you from all harm—he will watch over your life; the LORD will watch over your coming and going both now and forevermore. (Psalm 121:7–8)

Blessed are the people of whom this is true; blessed are the people whose God is the LORD. (Psalm 144:15)

The LORD is good to those whose hope is in him, to the one who seeks him. (Lamentations 3:25)

Whoever gives heed to instruction prospers, and blessed is he who trusts in the LORD. (Proverbs 16:20)

Delight yourself in the LORD and he will give you the desires of your heart. . . . If the LORD delights in a man's way, he makes his steps firm. (Psalm 37:4, 23)

Have no fear of sudden disaster or of the ruin that overtakes the wicked, for the LORD will be your confidence. (Proverbs 3:25–26)

God, by His very nature and by His command, deserves to be number one on my list.

ROLL CALL

Ultimately, everyone will give an account of himself to the Lord. "It is written: 'As surely as I live,' says the Lord, 'every knee will bow before me; every tongue will confess to God.' So then, each of us will give an account of himself to God" (Romans 14:11–12). No one will be exempt, whether or not God was number one on the person's list of priorities. In fact, even those who have failed to include Him at all will be accountable.

FOREVER AND EVER

My relationship with the Lord has eternal consequences.

That if you confess with your mouth, "Jesus is Lord," and believe in your heart that God raised him from the dead, you will be saved. (Romans 10:9)

It has eternal longevity.

Surely goodness and love will follow me all the days of my life, and I will dwell in the house of the LORD forever (Psalm 23:6)

As much as I love my husband, our relationship as husband and wife is only "till death do us part."

At the resurrection people will neither marry nor be given in marriage; they will be like the angels in heaven. (Matthew 22:30)

And as sweet and dear as my children are, they will establish their own families and I will have the privilege and honor of being an addendum to those families.

For this reason a man will leave his father and mother and be united to his wife, and they will become one flesh. (Genesis 2:24)

My relationship with the Lord will last for all of eternity.

All of these truths contributed to my choice to give God the number one spot on my list of priorities.

3

MY SECOND PRIORITY:
MY HUSBAND

The second item on my list of priorities is my husband, John. Our relationship, marriage, was the first union God created between human beings.

> The LORD God said, "It is not good for the man to be alone. I will make a helper suitable for him." . . . So the LORD God caused the man to fall into a deep sleep; and while he was sleeping, he took one of the man's ribs and closed up the place with flesh. Then the LORD God made a woman from the rib he had taken out of the man, and he brought her to the man. (Genesis 2:18, 21–22)

Putting John in spot number two on my list of priorities means that my relationship with the Lord will have a significant impact on my union with John. The number two position on the list is colored or influenced by position number one. How does that manifest itself? Ideally, I will allow God's instruction on marriage to guide my behavior. For example, God's Word says in Ephesians 5:22 that I, as a wife, am to submit to my husband "as to the Lord."

This portion of Scripture is often misunderstood. Submission does not mean to acquiesce in each and every situation and to give up thinking and learning and listening to God myself. Furthermore, it cannot mean to compromise God's instruction (for my interaction with John, my submission, is colored by God's loving position as number one in my life). Quite simply, submission means voluntary compliance.

I submit to the traffic light . . . stopping when it is red and continuing on when it is green. I voluntarily comply (and hope everyone else will too!).

I submit to the song leader at church as he requests that we stand and sing a hymn.

I submit to the flight attendant when she asks me to buckle my seat belt.

I submit to the election judge who requests my name.

I submit to my Sunday school teacher when he asks me to turn in my Bible to a certain Scripture.

I submit to the roller rink owner by skating in a clockwise direction (until told to do otherwise).

I submit to the checkout lady at the grocery store when she requests that I pay a certain amount for my groceries.

Submission is my choice. I choose when to comply and when not to comply. Why do I submit in all those situations listed above? Because all of those requests (and many others we could name) are reasonable and in some cases even act to protect me and others from harm. I submit, for submission is in my best interest.

Submission is only one part of the equation. In Ephesians 5:25 we read, "Husbands, love your wives, just as Christ loved the church and gave himself up for her." Submitting, voluntarily complying with a husband who is loving me "as Christ loved the church," is also in my best interest. It is reasonable and advantageous. In fact, it goes beyond reasonable and advantageous to become an exceptional blessing. It is not difficult to imagine voluntary compliance with someone displaying that kind of love. That is definitely in my best interest (as are all of God's commands).

A SUITABLE HELPER

Eve, the first wife, was considered by God to be a "suitable helper." A part of her role was to meet Adam's needs. The animals God had already created just didn't fit the bill. I want to be a suitable helper to my husband. I want to meet his needs. In order to do that, I must understand what his needs are. If our relationship is to grow and not stagnate—or worse—yet disintegrate, I need to strive to unselfishly meet John's needs.

Several years ago, John and I wrote an article about marriage for a nationwide periodical. It dealt with ministering to each other as a couple—meeting each other's needs. Shortly after it was published, I received a phone call from a reader. She was very distraught. Her marriage was dissolving, and her call was more one of lament than of inquiry.

I gently listened to her remorseful story, and one statement in her monologue shouted at me above all the others: "He never told me he had any needs. I didn't know he needed anything!"

Evidently the caller expected her husband to articulate his needs. This certainly is helpful, but it may or may not occur. Perhaps he *did* tell his wife his needs. Perhaps she chose to ignore the things he said. Whatever the situation, he *did* have needs, but now it was too late for his wife to meet them. Personally, I want to minister to John as the Lord suggests, submitting to him and meeting his needs as his suitable helper. John shouldn't have to demand it. Instead, it's my desire to respond to him and to his loving me as Christ loved the church.

POWERFUL RESULTS

By allowing God, my number one priority, to color my interaction with John, amazing things can happen. When we are operating according to the Word of God and being obedient to His instructions, our marriage relationship can produce some powerful, positive results. "If two of you on earth agree about anything you ask for, it will be done for you by my Father in heaven. For where two or three come together in my name, there am I with them" (Matthew 18:19–20).

By God's design, a Christian marriage is capable of not only blessing the partners, but others too.

TILL DEATH DO US PART

Ideally the marriage relationship is one of great longevity. My bond to God is eternal, and my kinship with John as his wife will continue throughout our time on earth. That is an important reason to cultivate, protect, and nurture our marriage, with God's Word as our guide.

HIS ORDER

Does God care that our spouse assumes second place on our list of priorities? Yes, I believe He does. Remember that God established the marriage relationship *after* He established the relationship between God and man. Then, after marriage was established, God gave Adam and Eve the command to "be fruitful and increase in number" (Genesis 1:28), and the parent/child relationship began. This original, God-ordained order, (1) bonding with God; (2) kinship with your spouse; and (3) connection with your children is the pattern I believe He wants us to continue to follow today.

4

MY THIRD PRIORITY:
MY CHILDREN

The next item on my list of priorities is my children. They are number three, following God and their father.

Years ago, Avis Rent-a-Car had an advertising campaign based on the theme "We're number two, but we try harder." At the time those commercials were on the air, only two major companies were renting cars, Hertz (who claimed to be number one) and Avis (who was "trying harder"). I'm assuming that what Avis was "trying harder" to do was to become number one.

Kids can be a lot like Avis. Although mine were given the number three position, many times they tried to move up in rank. Children do not like being preempted.

Recently I sat behind a three-year-old girl with her mother and her grandmother at a football game. At one point, the young girl wanted to tell her mother something. Unfortunately, her mom was having a conversation with grandma. I watched the little girl unsuccessfully attempt to interrupt the conversation, sigh loudly, try again (to no avail), and finally take her mother's face in her hands and literally turn her mom's attention to her. The little girl was tired of waiting for her mom's attention. She wanted it . . . she demanded it . . . right now!

I can remember this desire for my attention manifesting itself in my own kids. It almost always happened when the telephone rang.

THE LINE IS BUSY

Even if my children had been ignoring me up to that point in time, a ringing phone was like a magnet, drawing them to me. Does that ever happen in your home? The phone would ring and I would happily begin to chat with another adult. My boys, alerted by the ring of the phone, would encircle me, tangling themselves in the phone cord. Then they mouthed what initially appeared to be a desperate message, impossible to decipher. (By the way, don't even try to understand those impassioned pantomimes. I determined long ago that my kids—and probably your kids too—were saying absolutely nothing at all. It was all part of a plot to distract me and get my attention.) This predictable phone behavior occurred because the invisible person on the other end of the phone line had my attention.

That behavior is typical. A child might be able to understand coming after God on the list of priorities, but what in the world is Dad doing outranking them? Their insistent attitude and unarguable dependence in the early months and years of their lives can combine to move those little sweethearts ahead of Dad or maybe even ahead of the Lord on our lists.

Did/Do your children ever tug at your skirt and whine for your attention? I'm guessing the answer is yes. Did/Does your husband do the same? Mine never has. He is not that demanding. How about God? The answer is no again. The very fact that children are clamoring to move up in rank demands that I not casually overlook the priority order I have determined is best.

WET PAINT

In third position, my decisions about my children are colored by both numbers one and two . . . the Lord and their father. How does my relationship with God color my relationship with my children? Again, it is by the influence of His Word.

God tells us in Psalm 127:3b that children are "a reward from him." Even though there are days (or at least moments) when any parent would argue that classification, it is still true. Children are precious gifts from God. God wants us to develop parenting skills and to develop our relationship based on His Word.

Children are important members of God's family. Our responsibility to them is great.

And whoever welcomes a little child like this in my name welcomes me. But if anyone causes one of these little ones who believe in me to sin, it would be better for him to have a large millstone hung around his neck and to be drowned in the depths of the sea. (Matthew 18:5–6)

God cares about our relationship with our children. In the New Testament, Christ had to convince His disciples of the importance of children.

People were bringing little children to Jesus to have him touch them, but the disciples rebuked them. When Jesus saw this, he was indignant. He said to them, "Let the little children come to me, and do not hinder them, for the kingdom of God belongs to such as these." (Mark 10:13–14)

The Word of God is filled with verses reminding us that children are a blessing and teaching us principles of child rearing. God wants us to develop parenting skills and to develop our relationship with our kids based on His Word.

God encouraged the Israelite parents with these words: "Only be careful, and watch yourselves closely so that you do not forget the things your eyes have seen or let them slip from your heart as long as you live. Teach them to your children and to their children after them" (Deuteronomy 4:9).

God calls both father and mother to the task of parenting. Because of our differing genders and personalities, we bring different strengths to the task. Our agreement in the parenting process is essential. God's influence, coloring our marriage, gives us a strategy, and instruction, for raising loving, God-revering, confident children.

God's Word gives these instructions.

Fathers [and mothers], do not exasperate your children; instead, bring them up in the training and instruction of the Lord. (Ephesians 6:4)

The rod of correction imparts wisdom, but a child left to himself disgraces his mother. (Proverbs 29:15)

Fathers, do not embitter your children, or they will become discouraged. (Colossians 3:21)

Fix these words of mine in your hearts and minds; tie them as symbols on your hands and bind them on your foreheads. Teach them to your children, talking about them when you sit at home and when you walk along the road, when you lie down and when you get up. (Deuteronomy 11:18–19)

God gives instruction and He reveals great promises.

Train a child in the way he should go, and when he is old he will not turn from it. (Proverbs 22:6)

The righteous man leads a blameless life; blessed are his children after him. (Proverbs 20:7)

Praise the LORD. Blessed is the man who fears the LORD, who finds great delight in his commands. His children will be mighty in the land; each generation of the upright will be blessed. (Psalm 112:1–2)

A wise son brings joy to his father. (Proverbs 10:1)

All your sons will be taught by the LORD, and great will be your children's peace. (Isaiah 54:13)

Intentional parenting takes time and wisdom. As decisions are made from a strong basis—from the foundation of God's love and the love of husband and wife—the chances of success are greatly increased. And what is success? Raising children who honor God and their parents and have a healthy model for their possible roles as a spouse and parent someday. To do this, agreement between husband and wife is essential.

STICK TOGETHER

Presenting a united front in parenting is not always easy. Our children (all boys, remember) determined early on which parent to ask for permission in which circumstance. If the request involved some degree of daring, risk, or danger, they always approached their dad. He was much more likely to allow a solo ride on the horse or a run down a black diamond ski slope. (I would have been *sure* it was too dangerous.)

When it came to social events, however, they intelligently came to me. "Can I go to the pizza place with a bunch of kids after Bible study?" Because I am the social butterfly of their two parents, I could immediately see the potential fun in the outing and usually said yes. (Their dad would have wondered why they wanted to waste the time and energy.)

This division of labor in regard to granting permission is different from the situation when a child asks one parent, is denied the request, and then asks the other parent hoping for an override of the first ruling.

DANNY'S PLAN

On more than one occasion, Danny asked his dad if he could go here or there with this friend or that one. The initial answer was almost always no. Then he approached his mom with the same request. When asking her, he would mention that Dad had already vetoed the plan, but he would explain why that decision was not the best. Usually Mom felt sorry for Danny because Dad almost always said no without even considering the request. If Danny got a yes from Mom, he just accepted that answer and took advantage of the difference. If things exploded with Dad later, Danny vindicated himself by declaring his innocence as he had completely adhered to Mom's decision.

Finally, after repeated incidences of this, his parents decided to actually join forces in their child rearing. They decided to let their decisions about their children be colored by God and each other. They began to answer requests in light of God's Word and in agreement with each other.

One afternoon after school Danny asked his dad for permission to go to the junior high soccer game with a neighbor. Instead of his usual instantaneous "no," Dad evaluated the request. But because it was a school night and Danny needed to spend at least two hours doing homework, Dad wisely said no. No problem, Danny thought, and he approached Mom. When she asked, "What did your dad say?" Danny told her and was shocked to hear, "Then you can't go." This new parental plan was certainly not what Danny had hoped for, but it was one that strengthened his parents' relationship with each other and ultimately with him. Whenever possible, we should build our relationship with our children from a solid relationship with the Lord and our spouse.

BEING MATTHEW'S MOM

As moms, we run the great risk that we will allow our children to rank higher than our husbands on our priority list. Many times that is because we get a large portion of our identity from our kids. I remember the first time I was called "Matthew's mom." Chad, a preschool boy in Sunday school, had just made the connection between little baby Matthew and this lady—me. It sounded funny to me as a mother of a two-month-old baby. I knew about being "Kendra," and I had been called "Ruth and Noel's youngest" and "John's wife," but "Matthew's mom" was a new title. At that point and for years to come (eighteen to be exact), "Matthew's mom" was as much a job description as anything else. Being Matthew, Aaron, and Jonathan's mom described what I did each day. Now, as I write these words, my older two sons are in college and the youngest is in high school. The word "Mom" has made a considerable shift from job description to a term of endearment.

One of my goals is to raise godly, confident, independent young men, and a part of that independence will mean a separation from me. I want to cheer them on as they "leave and cleave," knowing that they have been an important priority in my life, but have not outranked their father or the Lord . . . my two best friends—one who will not leave me until death and One who will never leave me or forsake me (see Joshua 1:5).

5

MY FOURTH PRIORITY:
MY WORK

Just recently I served tea to a good friend of mine, Terri. She is an at-home mom and entrepreneur who works with me as my marketing director. We were meeting to discuss strategic planning, and in the meantime, we were talking about kids and church and schedules, etc. I have many mugs on hooks under the kitchen cabinets above my counter. As I scanned the possible mug selections, my eyes fell on the perfect one for Terri. The quote? "Every mother is a working mother!" How true!

I remember, with some disgust, a phrase that I heard repeatedly after I stopped teaching school. It went like this—"Now that you're not working . . ."

"Not working?!" I wanted to yell. "Have you ever tried to keep up with a two-year-old while suffering from sleep deprivation caused by the two-month-old?" *Every* mother is a working mother.

In addition to the obvious work associated with motherhood, some moms choose to work outside the home. And some choose to stay at home and work as home-based-business moms—this is the category of work we will examine for our discussions of "work."

As a home-based-business mom, I had to learn to discipline myself to limit my work in connection with my home-based business. Not only did I find a home-based business more fun than dusting; at times I wanted to use my work as an excuse to slack off in areas that were primary to my higher priorities. Even though John and my boys had achieved a higher ranking on my list, it was not always easy for me to keep things in perspective . . . to let numbers one through three color my decisions about my work, number four. (You'll read more about that battle.) Suffice it to say, work, no matter how much fun it is, is still ranked number four on my list of priorities.

I'M WORKING

It is very positive that I found my home-based business fun, but there is a risk in that. My son Aaron has a natural ability with horses, and that is his passion. After his freshman year in college, he decided to turn his passion into his summer profession. He put two ads in the *Thrifty Nickel*, and voilá—Aaron was in business, breaking and training horses and giving beginning riding lessons. And he loved it! I remember hearing my older brother talking to Aaron one day. He told him, "If you can figure out what you like to do, and find someone who will pay you to do it, you'll never work another day in your life." How true. The only risk is that because your work is so enjoyable, you may not always realize when you are working, and your work can begin to rise dangerously up the list of priorities.

When I began my home-based business I realized I had found a way to combine my passion for the Lord and for Christian books with my enthusiasm for sharing with others. When we love our work, it can be difficult to keep it in its rightful spot on the list of priorities. "Do I really need to make supper or go to the store or (yikes!) tuck the boys in? I'm working."

Work can move ahead of my kids, John, or even God if I become undisciplined. As I drove my eldest son, Matthew, home from campus after his first semester at college, I asked him how it felt to be *done*. After he expressed his relief (and the need for a good nap), I told him that his college years would probably be the last time he would feel he was "done." As an adult, we are never completely "done." Oh, one project or assignment may be complete—I may have changed all the sheets, finished the wash, or washed all the dishes—but undoubtedly someone will sleep, wear clothes, and eat again, and probably very soon! As a full-fledged adult, there is always an unending list of tasks to complete.

Multiply the typical never-ending list of jobs and activities by ten (or maybe more) when you are a home-based-business mom. You can always think of one more job to do . . . one more e-mail to send . . . one more adventure on which to embark. Colossians 3:23 says, "Whatever you do, work at it with all your heart, as working for the Lord, not for men." This verse says to work heartily, not work constantly.

God has set down some specific guidelines about work. We are not to work every day of the week. It is not a healthy choice, and it doesn't honor God. Furthermore, we receive several warnings from God.

> *For six days, work is to be done, but the seventh day shall be your holy day, a Sabbath of rest to the LORD. (Exodus 35:2a)*

> *Do not wear yourself out to get rich; have the wisdom to show restraint (Proverbs 23:4).*

> *Then he said to them, "Watch out! Be on your guard against all kinds of greed; a man's life does not consist in the abundance of his possessions." (Luke 12:15)*

> *For where your treasure is, there your heart will be also. (Luke 12:34)*

It is very important that our work be influenced by God and by His Word.

> *"Not by might nor by power, but by my Spirit," says the LORD Almighty. (Zechariah 4:6b)*

May the favor of the Lord our God rest upon us; establish the work of our hands for us—yes, establish the work of our hands. (Psalm 90:17)

Unless the LORD builds the house, its builders labor in vain. (Psalm 127:1a)

No one wants to labor in vain, and God will see to it that we do not suffer that malady if we honor Him.

Have you ever heard the phrase "The hurrier I go the behinder I get"? We do not have to hurry or panic or devote time away from our better priorities or the best in order to achieve success in our home-based business.

A LESSON LEARNED

I learned the lesson about not having to be panicky and torn in all directions the hard way. When I started my home-based business I discovered many things about myself. One of those things was that I responded enthusiastically to competition and even more so to prizes. Hold a carrot in front of me, and I will run as fast as I can to capture it (oftentimes ignoring more important responsibilities). There were times in the early years of my home-based business when John literally asked me what the particular prize was in a company-wide contest I was considering entering. Then he offered to award me that same prize if I *did not* enter the contest. (That should have been a clue, shouldn't it?)

Every year at the convention of the direct sales company I was affiliated with, recognition was given to the person who had sponsored the most distributors. Each month the statistics were published in the newsletter, and one year I was consistently in the lead. In fact, after a few months of leading the pack, I made it my goal to finish the year on top. I pursued that goal with gusto—spending time with my work that should have been spent on my more important priorities.

Finally, it was time for the convention. And the winner was named! It was . . . (drumroll) . . . not me! I was in the number two position (and there was no prize for that). I was immediately disappointed—not so much because I didn't win the prize, but because I realized that I had allowed my priorities to become jumbled. Before the evening was over, I vowed to get first things first and to take those commitments much more seriously. And, incredibly, I did. The pain of realizing the error of my way was a great motivator. I renewed my determination to let each preceding priority color those that followed.

And would you believe it? At the next year's convention, I received an award of achievement. Burning the candle at both ends, putting work ahead of the better and the best, did not bring a desirable end. Keeping my balance, with my priorities where they belonged, was rewarded.

COMPROMISE PRIORITIES?

My home-based business shifted from the direct sale of Christian books by various popular authors to professional speaking and writing books myself. Because of my home-based-business background, I found that I was being contacted to speak to sales forces who were mostly home-based-business moms. I am just as comfortable with these audiences as I am in a church retreat setting. I am mindful, however, that the individuals in attendance cannot be presumed to be Christians. (Actually, I'm foolish to ever presume that.) I am aware that I have been contracted to speak from my expertise in the area of home-based business and not my expertise (?) on the Word of God.

I had been dialoguing with one particular home-based business about the possibility of speaking at their national convention. The convention director was very enthusiastic, and she requested that I send a video to give her an idea of my style. Without a great deal of thought, I sent her a video of a message I had successfully given to another home-based business. In that message, I enumerated my priorities, beginning, of course, with the Lord.

A week later I contacted the convention director to see if a decision had been made. The conversation began with these words: "I really don't think you will be a good fit with our company." I was shocked! One week before, she had all but issued a contract. What had happened in the meantime?

When I asked her why she had that opinion, she offered three reasons. The first two were very weak and I was able to present a plausible solution to both. Then she got to the crux of the problem. "Well," she began, "I think that you are too religious for our company." (I had already begun to suspect that perception was the real problem.)

At that point I had a decision to make. The first two objections she had presented were very fixable. But "too religious"? I decided that was *not* something that needed to be fixed.

"I am a Christian," I replied. "There is no changing that. The message you heard on the video was one that included, by necessity, the noting of that fact. Many of my other messages are not directly related to my faith. You may feel free to select any message you feel would best benefit your company. I will not force my beliefs on anyone else. Instead, it is my goal to be the fragrance of Christ. That will not change."

And to my surprise her reply was "I don't believe the way you do, but I genuinely respect your commitment to that belief. I think we *will* be able to work together."

How about that? It's true. It is important that we establish our priorities and do our utmost to live with each ranking priority coloring those down the page.

6

MY FIFTH PRIORITY:
OTHER GOOD THINGS

The fifth priority on my list I simply call "other good things." This category is very broad. It spans VBS cookies, PTA offices, choir solos, field trip chaperoning, carpool organizing, and much more. Extended family and friendships also fall under this heading. The "other good things" are very hard to keep in balance because they are just that—they are good!

"Kendra, can you solicit workers for the school carnival?"

"Kendra, would you mind baking another three dozen cookies for the conference at church?"

"Kendra, we'd like you to consider being PTA president."

And what do I say?

"OK."

"Alright."

"I guess so."

Even though at the age of two our favorite word was no, we have somehow forgotten that, and now we agree to almost everything . . . at least to every good thing.

If anyone ever dared to call me and say, "Kendra, we have a dastardly deed we're planning, and we wondered if you could help," I would be quick to say no. But that doesn't happen. It's all those "other good things."

I remember my friend telling me about the time she volunteered to sew forty vests for the Bible club. What a good thing! Well, she went on to tell me that as she sewed the vests, she screamed at her own four children. She had said yes to something good and had sacrificed something better.

MOM GOES TO CAMP

Years ago I was the speaker at a summer church camp entitled "Mom Goes to Camp." One complete session was devoted to the topic of establishing priorities. When I suggested that "other good things" appear in the fifth position, being colored or influenced by numbers one through four, one woman looked obviously troubled. When the time rolled around for questions, her hand shot up immediately.

"Do you mean," she inquired, "that even if the church asks me to do something, I have the option of saying no?"

Yes, indeed, that was precisely what I meant to communicate. "The answer, yes or no, does not depend on *who* is asking. It depends on how the request fits into your life and your list of priorities," I replied. "If saying yes to baking more VBS cookies shortchanges your work, your children, your spouse, or the Lord, then yes is the wrong answer."

"I am a teacher and a wife and a mom," she continued, a little teary-eyed. "This may seem naive, but whenever someone called from the church with a request, I somehow thought that saying no would disappoint God. I hate to think of how many times I've said yes (for all the wrong reasons) and then have ignored all four of my top priorities to get the job done. This is a truly liberating thought!"

For weeks I waited for hate mail from all the committee chairmen at her church. Thankfully I never received any. This lovely, well-educated professional was confusing God and "other good things." That can easily happen.

LET'S GO!

"Other good things" are not only responsibilities. Sometimes they are merely things we *want* to do. Unfortunately, I have an all too recent, vivid example in my own life.

Last spring I got excited about attending a two-day conference featuring a very good Bible teacher. I got so excited, in fact, that I was able to motivate a whole van full of women to sign up for the conference too. We were scheduled to travel to Nashville for three days in early December.

Even though I attend many women's retreats each year, the idea of being in the *audience* of a conference with several of my favorite girlfriends was very appealing. We sent the money for the tickets, and we were committed. Many times throughout the summer and fall I rejoiced with anticipation as I thought about our outing.

Early in the fall I began to have respiratory problems. The diagnoses included bronchitis, allergies, pneumonia, and laryngitis. These different diagnoses were all accompanied by prescriptions. The entire diagnostic process (moving from bronchitis to laryngitis) took three months. Basically I was under the weather the entire time. I was able to do what was nonnegotiable, but spent a lot of time resting.

As the time for the women's conference drew nearer, I was determined to get well and head to Nashville with my girlfriends. Unfortunately the last diagnosis occurred on the Monday before the Thursday departure. My doctor ruled that, although I was not particularly contagious, I should rest and, more important, I should *not* talk . . . not even a whisper!

Ridiculously optimistic, I followed orders pretty well on Monday, Tuesday, and Wednesday. By Wednesday night I was still hoping for some miraculous intervention. I didn't feel bad enough to stay home, and yet I wasn't sure I could go to the conference and obey my doctor's orders.

On Tuesday night I had had a difficult time sleeping. On Wednesday evening I realized that I needed to be decisive. Could I really go on Thursday and not risk my health? Did I have to miss this conference that I had been looking forward to for so long?

As I prepared for bed that night I prayed for wisdom. In the back of my mind I thought I might have a terrible night's sleep and then would know for sure that traveling was out of the question. That would definitely give me my answer, but the thought of coughing and tossing and turning was exhausting in itself. So I added a little addendum to my prayer for wisdom. "And could You let me know if it's best for me to stay home some way other than a sleepless night?"

That night was very restful—surprisingly so. In fact, I slept like a rock, and so did John. We ignored the alarms and the fact that dawn was breaking. I awoke with a start about an hour and a half *after* my body alarm usually sounds. It was already seven o'clock. I had slept well, but the time I had allowed to shower and pack (just in case the wise answer was "Go") had completely vanished. I woke John, who usually rises even earlier than I do, put on my sweatshirt and sweatpants, and went to church to tell my sweet girlfriends "Godspeed." Was I disappointed? Yes! Was I devastated? No. That "other good thing" would not have been good for my health. And good health is a necessity to my work and my family.

The "other good thing" was so tempting, but it had to be evaluated and colored by the priorities ahead of it on my list. I couldn't go *this* time, but maybe next time. "Other good things" must stay in their place. You just can't do it all.

THE DO-IT-ALL MYTH

A mom told me that before she had her first child and became a home-based-business mom, she always thought that only women who worked outside the home had to deal with the myth that they could do it all. Then she joined the home-based-business ranks and discovered the same myth was alive and well in the lives of those working at home. We *want* to do it all, including the fun stuff, but we cannot. Philippians 4:13 says, "I can do everything through him who gives me strength." It does not say we *are* to do everything. Instead, we are to attribute our abilities and strength to our source, to God.

Every woman, every mom, must make choices. In one sense, home-based-business moms have more choices to make because the mom working outside the home has relinquished some of her choices to others. Her schedule, work time, and deadlines are often controlled by someone else. As a home-based-business mom, you must make choices about all of those things and many others. The choice of a home-based business opens the door to many more choices, including the choice of which "other good things" are to be accepted and which are to be rejected. Allowing your list of priorities to be painted in watercolors with numbers one through four coloring your decision about position number five will help.

TIME INVESTMENT

I look at this list like a target on the wall. Being the mother of sons, I have engaged in many dart games through the years. I do not tell you this to brag about my ability to hurl little pointed objects toward a target with great accuracy. In fact, I don't have great accuracy. Occasionally I do hit the bull's-eye, but on many more occasions, I do not even hit the target. The good news about having a target, however, is that it assures I will be facing the right wall!

By listing my priorities, by painting them with watercolors, I create a target. I may not always hit the bull's-eye, but at least I'm facing the right wall!

PART TWO:

KNOWING WHAT YOU'RE DOING AND WHY

"I must honestly define and delineate all facets of my various 'jobs.'"

7

ESTABLISHING YOUR "JOBS" DESCRIPTION:
YOUR TIME COMMITMENT

What a strange title for a section of this book—"Knowing What You're Doing and Why"! Don't you already know what you're doing (or contemplating doing) in your home-based business and why you're doing it?

If you are a home-based-business editor, you edit. Right? If you're a home-based-business mom in direct sales, you sell. Right? A home-based-business hairdresser fixes hair in her home. A home-based-business seamstress sews. This is not difficult. So why did I choose to dedicate an entire heading to "knowing what you're doing and why"? Perhaps (no, most certainly) it is because when I first started my home-based business, the direct sale of Christian books, I did not actually know the answer to that question.

When I admit my ignorance, it's important for you to under-stand what I mean. I understood the basics of the business plan. And

I was very familiar with the product since both my husband and I enjoyed reading. That was not where I was lacking. What I did not know was how to honestly evaluate why I was involved in my home-based business and the time commitment I should make to my work.

I've already admitted to you that I love contests and prizes. When I first started in my home-based business, I jumped into it with all my energy. In fact, I was way out of balance and dangerously close to falling from the high wire. My priorities were jumbled, and I had not taken the time to honestly evaluate what I was doing. I assumed that my work was on a level plane with my husband's and that because of that equality it was legitimate to expect that he would assume equal responsibility in our household. The problem with that premise was that I was not working to contribute to the financial security of the family (one of his primary responsibilities). Instead you may recall that I was largely motivated by adult interaction and by acquiring relief from some minor household responsibilities.

If I was ever to balance my life as a home-based-business mom, it was imperative that I identify, honestly, what I was doing and why I was doing it. I needed to define the purpose and the motivation of my home-based business. In the next few chapters we'll look at some possible motivations, and then we'll spend a few more chapters considering how the various aspects of a home-based-business mom's life fit together.

All a man's ways seem innocent to him, but motives are weighed by the LORD. (Proverbs 16:2)

8

GAINING PERSONAL FULFILLMENT

Many people are hesitant to admit that their involvement in any particular activity is motivated by the need for personal fulfillment. How could I need/choose a home-based business to aid my personal fulfillment when I had a wonderful husband and a healthy, happy child? What was wrong with me? Absolutely nothing.

As a school teacher, I found a lot of satisfaction in working with my students and other members of the staff. In fact, I received many compliments and accolades while teaching. That is not always the case in motherhood.

On one particular occasion when I was feeling a little under-appreciated as a mother and wife, my sweet husband generously summarized my dilemma. "It's like this," he explained. "Part of your 'job' as a mom is to see to it that everyone else's life runs smoothly. And, frankly, you do that so well that no one notices."

What a wise (and kind) analysis! Part of being a mom, that daily part, often goes unnoticed. When was the last time your son or daughter thanked you for clean socks or a nutritious breakfast? But leave something undone or serve peanut butter and jelly sandwiches one too many times in a week and you'll hear from them.

"My uniform isn't washed yet?" a child might ask incredulously. "What have you been doing all day?"

The tasks of motherhood are often unappreciated. And they are so *daily*. I wouldn't mind cooking if they didn't just rush in and eat it. Then I've got to do it all over again. And the laundry is never done. People continually wear clothes. There's just no reprieve.

And so I found that a home-based business was capable of bolstering my self-esteem and contributing to my fulfillment. In Dr. James Dobson's best-seller *What Wives Wish Their Husbands Knew About Women*, he dedicated an entire chapter to the subject of low self-esteem in women.

> Believe it or not, *Low Self-Esteem* was indicated as *the* most troubling problem by the majority of the women completing the questionnaire. More than 50 percent of the group marked this item above every other alternative on the list, and 80 percent placed it in the top five. This finding is perfectly consistent with my own observations and expectations: even in seemingly healthy and happily married young women, personal inferiority and self-doubt cut the deepest and leave the most wicked scars.[1]

Low self-esteem is at nearly epidemic proportions among women. And for many, the establishment of a home-based business can act to reverse that epidemic while keeping priorities in order. A home-based business can be adapted to the responsibilities of motherhood and the needs of children and home.

A PRESCRIPTION

Years ago I attended a meeting for my direct sales home-based business. At this meeting, people were given an opportunity to tell something they appreciated about their business. To my surprise, one of the people to approach the microphone was a gentleman whose wife was active in the business. His role was entirely a supportive one.

When it was his turn to speak, his words went something like this: "I have personally observed the positive things this home-based business has done for my wife," he began. "She thoroughly enjoys the people she has met and the opportunity she has had to positively influence people's lives. It has made a wonderful impact on her. After all, you can't go to the drugstore and buy eight ounces of self-esteem."

In other words, he felt strongly that his wife's home-based business had contributed positively to her self-esteem. There is nothing wrong with focusing on this aspect of having a home-based business.

MY JOB DESCRIPTION

When I finally identified personal fulfillment as my primary reason for my home-based business, I had to take an honest look at many things. First of all, I realized that I could not use my home-based business as an excuse to dodge the daily tasks of motherhood or home-making or housekeeping. Sure, I could get out of dusting, but things like the meals and the laundry and cleaning were still largely my responsibility. John had a very full plate with his job(s), and although I was contributing to the income (OK, *slightly* contributing to the income . . . OK, OK, my business was not costing John anything. See what I mean about being honest? It's tough sometimes.) . . . Anyway, when I honestly evaluated my job as providing personal fulfillment, I could hardly expect John to assume many of my responsibilities. He was willing to provide me with child-free times to devote to business, but he could not/would not allow me to unfairly (and dishonestly) claim "work" as an excuse to dodge unpleasant tasks.

TRUTH SERUM

Did you happen to notice how many times the words *honest* and *honestly* appeared as I acknowledged the true job description/motivation of my home-based business? It's hard to admit, but it was very difficult for me to be honest about what I was doing. For whatever reason, I wanted to give my work what I saw as a higher status. Please understand that my roles as a wife and mom cannot genuinely be topped by any other role. But, again being honest, there were times, days even, that that very true, very accurate concept evaded me.

I was a teenager in the late 1960s and early '70s when women were (gag) finding themselves, declaring their equality, and genuinely striving to mess up future generations. In my collegiate experience at a Big Ten University, I was inundated with the idea that women who chose to be at-home mothers (or mothers at all) were somehow either substandard or terribly confused. At the very least, they were not fulfilling their potential.

So when I chose to be an at-home mom, I felt that my home-based business *should* be bringing in revenue. It *should* be something significant. It *should* be providing something more than just personal fulfillment. I had to take a shot of sodium pentathol, the truth serum, and face the facts. What was the truth? (1) My home-based business was a wonderful, healthy diversion from some of the dailyness of being a mom and a homemaker. (2) I did not earn a substantial amount of money and hence could not expect my husband to ignore his work to pick up my slack. (3) Being involved in a home-based business for the purpose of personal fulfillment was absolutely fine. I did not need to fantasize or rationalize that my home-based business, at that point, was anything more.

After a big dose of honest evaluation, I was able to enjoy the fact that my home-based business met some of my needs and bolstered my self-esteem. That admission made the daily tasks of being a mom and a homemaker more enjoyable. My home-based business provided some much desired appreciation, encouraged me, and gave me confidence in my very real commitment to my family.

NOTE

1. James Dobson, *What Wives Wish Their Husbands Knew About Women* (Wheaton, Ill.: Tyndale, 1975), 22.

EARNING
SUPPLEMENTAL INCOME

By now you've probably decided whether or not you can define the primary motivation in your home-based business as personal fulfillment. If that is not applicable to you, perhaps your emphasis is supplemental income.

Providing supplemental income for your family usually takes one of two distinct forms. It is possible that the income you generate will be used to help meet your family's monthly budget. It may be earmarked to pay the electric bill or to buy groceries. It may be a necessary addition to your income, making it possible to meet your family's basic needs. Or the supplemental income you earn may be applied to things like family vacations or "luxuries" (by loose definition) not necessarily in your budget. Either option is legitimate and would qualify your income as supplemental.

It is important to know what you're doing, because it helps you to determine your time commitment to your work—your home-based business. Hopefully you have already established your time investment by determining your list of priorities. Now by defining your job description you can determine the time commitment that is required. If your supplemental income is helping meet your family's budget requirements, you will have to devote an adequate amount of time to earn the necessary amount.

SUPPLEMENTING OUR INCOME

At one point in the history of my home-based business, my emphasis shifted from personal fulfillment to supplemental income. My husband had also "retired" from teaching and was now farming and flying for the U.S. Air Force Reserves. As farmers, we witnessed the effect of a summer drought on our crops. I needed to get a little more serious about my time commitment in order to earn enough to help meet our budget needs.

How much time did I need to devote to my home-based business? How much time could my family tolerate (or actually encourage)? How could John and the boys help to fill in gaps that might be created by increasing my time commitment to my home-based business? John and I had to look honestly (there's that important word again) at what amount of work could potentially produce the money necessary to supplement our diminished family income.

At that point in time, my home-based business was the direct sale of Christian books. I had begun to do some speaking, but it was not a significant amount. And I had not begun to write professionally. As the definition of my home-based business shifted from personal fulfillment to necessary supplemental income, we first had to determine how much I would need to earn to meet our budget. After that, we made an estimate of how many book shows would be required to meet that need—based on the average income a typical show produced.

Each day was divided into three units . . . morning, afternoon, and evening. We determined that it would potentially take three units doing a book party away from home each week to produce the money necessary to supplement our income and meet our needs. Because he was no longer teaching and had a flexible schedule, John was able to be in charge of the boys and the basic household responsibilities for those three units each week. Beyond that, I would be home and work around the boys' schedule when I needed to make calls or process orders. Three units produced enough income to fill the gaps, and John was willing to help with some of my responsibilities.

FINANCIAL SECURITY

Dr. Willard Harley proposed an interesting theory in his book *His Needs, Her Needs*. He discussed a woman's need for financial security and the use of the wife's supplemental income to meet basic family needs.

Whatever women say in public about their willingness to share the burden of making a living, in private I hear something entirely different. Married women tell me they resent working, if their working is an absolute necessity. Even part-time work sometimes irritates them if their income has to help pay for basic living expenses.[1]

Remember that this is Dr. Harley's observation. For our family, my home-based business assumed the role of supplying need-meeting income for only a few months. Because of that short duration I am unable to personally reflect on Dr. Harley's premise. My home-based business helped to meet our family's budget needs for several months and then evolved to provide supplemental income for things that could not be classified as needs. That is the other option for the supplemental income category.

SHIRLEY'S STORY

My friend Shirley began her home-based business with a specific goal in mind—to provide a certain "luxury" for her family. Shirley had seen a beautiful oak table and buffet at the furniture store and knew that it did not fit into their single-income family budget.

So she decided to earn the specific amount of money needed to buy the table. That was her motivation for beginning a home-based business, and she was not sure if she would continue to work after the table and buffet were purchased.

I didn't discover a dining room table that caught my fancy, but I soon began to set aside the profit from my home-based business for family vacations and for incidentals we could definitely live without if necessary.

An added bonus that I discovered when I increased my productivity and my earnings was the joy and opportunity to increase my giving. By taking my home-based business a little more seriously, and managing my business more professionally, I had more to give to the ministries we supported.

When the emphasis of my home-based business shifted from supplemental income that was necessary to meet our budget needs to supplemental income providing "luxuries," I could no longer assume that John was willing to contribute his time and energy to cover a portion of my responsibilities. Again we had to evaluate the importance of those "luxuries." A common trap experienced by many families today is to fail to be satisfied or content without more and more. Don't allow that to happen to you. Ask yourself: "How much is enough?" If you are stumped by that question or if the answer is always "Just a little more . . ." reevaluate your motivation.

Many times it became necessary for me to adjust my fast track timetable to the needs of my better priority items.

WORKING TOGETHER BETTER

Throughout my history as a home-based-business mom, I have witnessed the importance of working with my husband. "Working together" doesn't imply that John has ever been directly involved with my business. He has not, but he has always been on my imaginary "board of directors." Since our family is very high on my list of priorities, John is in a good position to help me honestly evaluate whether my priorities are in order and to suggest when adjustments are necessary. Effectively working together, however, demands good communication. Let's take a look at the "breadwinner" home-based-business definition, and then we'll examine the aspect of good communication.

NOTE

1. Willard F. Harley Jr., *His Needs, Her Needs* (Grand Rapids: Revell, 1986, 1994), 122.

10

BEING THE BREADWINNER

Perhaps you are the breadwinner and a home-based-business mom. There can be a multitude of reasons for this distinction. Perhaps you are widowed or divorced. Maybe your husband is unable to work, or possibly you have assumed untraditional roles. Whatever the reason, when a home-based-business mom is the breadwinner, she obviously has a tremendous amount of responsibility to earn income.

It is possible that, before considering a home-based business, you were already classified as the breadwinner, winning that bread by some means other than a home-based business. If that is the case for you now, I would recommend that you do not make any sudden changes. "Don't quit your day job" is very sound advice. If you are contemplating a home-based business, working for yourself and being a business owner/entrepreneur, you need to know that there are risks involved. In fact, the very definition of an entrepreneur is someone who owns her own business and assumes the risk for the sake of the profit.

THE EXTRA PRESSURES INVOLVED

If you are the adult solely responsible for meeting the budget needs of your family, it is important you weigh the consequences and the risk of starting your own business. An entrepreneurial enterprise might be a little too unpredictable.

If, as the breadwinner, you give a home-based business a try without "quitting your day job," you run another risk—that of shortchanging your important priorities. You will be adding additional time commitments to your already busy day. It is hard to imagine doing this without depriving your higher ranking priorities, unless you have a tremendous amount of support—both emotional and physical. If that is the situation, you may be able to test the waters with the addition of a home-based business. Again, you will need to do an honest evaluation of the time commitment.

A full-time home-based business, providing the necessary income for a family to live, obviously requires a serious commitment of time, energy, and probably ingenuity. Being a home-based-business mom in order to support your family is one option. The demanding time commitment of your work will make your balancing act more difficult, but not impossible.

SHE WON THE BREAD

Rosey was a single mom, separated from her husband and raising three children. Not only did her husband fail to pay child support, but he had run up excessive debt before he deserted his family.

Because Rosey's children were young and none of her extended family lived close, she decided that her best option was to become a home-based-business mom. She was a very talented seamstress, able to make drapes with her heavy-duty sewing machine. So Rosey made arrangements with a department store to make their custom draperies. She was able to be home with her children except when measurements needed to be taken. Then she loaded everyone into the car and they all went along, sitting quietly while their mother measured and took notes.

Rosey was able to provide for her family's needs and actually whittle away at the debt her estranged husband had accrued.

Needless to say, three units of time outside my home and borrowed minutes of paperwork and booking inside my home would not have been sufficient to meet all the needs of our family. I have never been the breadwinner for our family, but with good planning and adequate time commitment, a home-based-business mom can potentially accept this responsibility and be successful.

11

THE NEED FOR
GOOD COMMUNICATION

ON THE SAME TEAM

Before our children arrived I coached girls' basketball. At the same time, John was coaching boys' basketball. We did not, however, teach in the same school districts. On Monday through Friday mornings, we both headed for school. He traveled about twelve miles north and I traveled about twenty-five miles south. His basketball team wore red jerseys and mine wore blue. But in spite of our busy schedules (or perhaps because of them), we knew the importance of wearing the *same* color jerseys in our married life. We learned from an early time that it is not healthy, profitable, or enjoyable to compete in marriage. Each of us brings different strengths and weaknesses. By working together, we can eliminate some of our weaknesses and capitalize on our strengths.

If you are married and a home-based-business mom, it is very important for you and your spouse to "wear the same color jersey." Working together is extremely significant. And one key to working together is good communication and honest discussion.

KNOWING AND DOING

Knowing how important it is to have good communication and *having* good communication are really two different things. I'm almost positive I have always known that good communication is important, and I'm equally positive that on more than one occasion I have failed in that category when it came to my home-based business. In fact, John and I have had to learn the art of good communication as it has applied to my business. And, truthfully, we are still perfecting it.

I have already mentioned the importance of honestly evaluating the purpose or motivation behind your home-based business. This can be accomplished more effectively if you and your husband work together to define the motivation. I have witnessed many a home-based-business mom (present company included) who was not interested in dialoguing, in genuinely communicating, with her husband about the motivation behind her home-based business. There were undoubtedly many reasons for this reluctance, but I have discovered that often it was the desire to hide the true motivation—even if it was at the expense of the family or the home-based business itself.

What if I admit that I am starting a home-based business to avoid dusting and to interact with other women? What if my husband says that those are not good reasons? What if I offend my husband by suggesting that he is unable to meet our family's needs? What if he demands a certain monetary contribution to the family when I want to use my income for discretionary things?

All these fears and many others can intimidate women and dissuade them from talking honestly with their husbands about the dreams, desires, and determinations they have for their home-based businesses. By protecting these intangibles, the potential support of your spouse is lost, and so is any chance for his helpful input. A better plan? Good communication.

Initially I was not eager to dialogue with John about my home-based business. I too feared that I would lose control and he would not see my motivation as valid. I thought he might not encourage me in my business or, worse, that he would discourage my interest. Early on I tried to guess what he would consider a viable motivation or description of the purpose of my home-based business. I imagined that he would only appreciate a business that produced supplemental income, so I tried to convince him that increased income would result from the time I was committing to my work. This plan was only effective until I showed *no* significant income. At that point, he resented the time I had spent with my business and the time he had spent assuming a portion of my responsibilities. We were not experiencing good communication (to say the least). I was afraid that, if I was honest with him, my real motivation wouldn't measure up and he might pressure me to walk away from my home-based business.

So what happened to push us toward honest communication? It was the desire we both had to be working together—even in this thing called a home-based business. The discussions (sometimes lengthy) began as we worked to achieve good communication in this aspect of our lives too.

The Hidden Agenda

Instead, speaking the truth in love . . . (Ephesians 4:15)

The first communication problem we tackled was the issue of a hidden agenda. This is a definite roadblock to good communication. A hidden agenda is used by someone when he or she consciously or unconsciously determines that the underlying truth—the true agenda—must be disguised in order to be achieved. A surface presentation (usually untrue or at best only somewhat accurate) is perceived as more appropriate, powerful, or acceptable. The purpose of the surface presentation is to mask the real truth.

My surface presentation suggested that the motivation of my home-based business was to provide supplemental income for our family. The underlying truth was that I had begun my home-based business with the idea of acquiring personal fulfillment. I hid my true agenda in order to gain John's approval and encouragement in my endeavor. I masked my true motivation and (gulp) furnished an untrue surface presentation.

As is usually the case, a hidden agenda doesn't stay hidden for long. When my surface presentation failed to materialize, I was forced to reveal my underlying truth—my hidden agenda. (Which, obviously, was then no longer hidden.) Although this revelation was not necessarily a pleasant task, it opened the door for better communication. It is very difficult to have good communication if either partner has a hidden agenda. With my true agenda finally in the open, we were able to move forward in our communication about my home-based business.

Another Communication Quirk

Do not merely listen to the word, and so deceive yourselves. Do what it says. (*James* 1:22)

A hidden agenda was not the only communication roadblock we encountered. After we began to honestly dialogue about my true agenda and motivation, I realized that my words and my actions were not always in sync. This is a definite hindrance to good communication.

In our discussions about my home-based business I would wholeheartedly agree with John that it was important for me to adjust my schedule for home-based-business work around his work schedule. After all, he was the breadwinner. I had no problem verbally endorsing this proposition. My words told him I understood and was willing to do what we both agreed was the most sensible thing in light of my job description, the time commitment, and his responsibilities.

Then, in direct conflict to my words, I would book an event without checking his schedule, hoping somehow it might work out. My words said, "I understand; I'll schedule around your schedule." My actions were in direct contrast. And, of course, my actions spoke louder than my words.

I am certain that everyone reading this book speaks English. I have no idea if any of you are bilingual. No, wait. That's not true. I know you speak English *and* Body Language. Actually, to be more accurate, you speak English and you *shout* Body Language. Actions speak louder than words. Our actions can be obvious or sublime, but they contribute mightily to our communication. One researcher even suggested that words are only a small part of what we communicate. In 1967, Professor Albert Mehrabian determined that "55% of the message a person receives is nonverbal . . . 38% is based on tone . . . and only 7% is our actual words."[1]

When I told John I understood the importance of honoring his schedule, he heard 45 percent of the message (my tone and words). My actions (in direct contrast to my words) spoke louder. It didn't matter what I had said.

So . . . after I became aware of the discrepancy between my words and my actions, I made a more concerted effort to put the two into agreement. And our communication improved once again.

I'm Listening

He who has ears, let him hear. (Matthew 11:15)

Sometimes our incongruent words and actions are the result of poorly developed listening skills. Listening is a very important skill in good communication. God gave us two ears and one mouth, a ratio that probably should not be ignored. In fact His Word says we should be "quick to listen, slow to speak and slow to become angry" (James 1:19).

Improving listening skills is a universal need. It does not just apply to the marriage partnership in regard to a home-based business. In a recent newspaper question-and-answer feature called "Working Wounded," Bob Rosner received a question from a worker who had been informed by his boss that he needed to improve his listening skills. "Well," he commented in his letter to Rosner, "I heard THAT!"[2]

Better listening is essential to good communication. One aspect of becoming a better listener is to try to do away with preconceived notions about what the speaker is saying. I have an acquaintance who is a very good speaker. He is a professor at a theological seminary and also a seminar speaker. I once heard him preface a message with these words: "First of all, I want to tell you what I'm going to say. And then I'm going to say it. After that, I'll tell you again what I said and also what I didn't say. If I don't, you may only listen to the point of your bias."

Now I'm sure he didn't give that introduction every time, but his point was well taken. We can easily hear only what we want to hear (even if it wasn't said at all).

In order to communicate with John about my home-based business, I had to develop better listening skills and hear what was being said, not just what I wanted to hear. But how can this be done? One help is to give the speaker your full attention. Many times we let our minds wander. Maintaining eye contact with the speaker can help. As Bob Rosner points out,

> Often, when we think we're listening to the OTHER person, we're really listening to OURSELVES: We're rehearsing the argument we're going to use to refute them, or we're jumping to conclusions off the first point they made, or we're revving up some other point to use whether it's relevant or not.[3]

Another trap of poor listening is to listen to only a portion of the message. My father had a standard line he used time after time when I would attempt to explain something to him—something he didn't wish to hear. Midway through the explanation, he would jokingly raise his hand to stop my talking and say, "Don't confuse me with the facts; my mind is made up." Cute, but not good for communication. "He who answers before listening—that is his folly and his shame" (Proverbs 18:13).

You can also become a better listener by asking relevant questions or by reiterating what has been said. Bob Rosner said, "Restate what you heard the person say. This has three benefits: It shows her that you're listening; it gives her a chance to correct misunderstandings; and it reinforces her points in your mind."[4]

Listening is an art that can be developed and refined. And ultimately whether or not you have listened well will be evaluated by what you do. If I have actually learned or understood something through my listening, it will manifest itself in a change of behavior. That is, after all, the simplest definition of learning.

John's Turn

Therefore encourage one another and build each other up, just as in fact you are doing. (1 Thessalonians 5:11)

I wasn't the only one contributing to our poor communication in the area of my home-based business. Another communication roadblock can occur when one partner fails to express the positive in a situation.

Do you know someone who is perpetually negative, seldom complimentary or encouraging, with a tendency to whine or complain? Is it you? If it is, you are not contributing to good communication.

It is very difficult to communicate when one partner seems to be constantly looking for (and finding) the negative in a situation. When that is the case, we become defensive and tend to turn off and tune out.

Initially, John felt it was his duty to point out the negative aspects of my home-based business—just in case I had missed them. The more "realistic" he became, the more "Pollyanna" I became—trying to negate the negatives. Both behaviors were reactions to each other. We were trying to counteract each other. Neither attitude was 100 percent correct.

When it came to my home-based business, John had to learn to express the positive. It wasn't that he didn't believe there were positive things to celebrate; he simply failed to express them, and good communication was hindered.

CONVERSATION TURN-OFFS

There was one particular communication roadblock that both of us could (and did) execute. We had each developed particular communication turn-offs that we used whenever we desired to shut down the lines of communication. Many of these are available, but we each had our favorite.

My particular favorite was "Boo Hoo Hoo!" (the manipulative use of crying). I'll never forget when my dear husband discovered that my tears had an ulterior motive. We had been debating some issue (which one, I don't remember), and I began to cry. John gently reached over and patted me and said these words (which I *do* remember): "I can understand why you're upset. And you just go ahead and cry. And when you're done, we'll continue our discussion." I distinctly remember thinking that I might as well stop because my tears were obviously not going to make any difference. They were not going to stop the conversation—at least not permanently. The jig was up!

John's favorite communication turn-off was not tears. His sounded something like this:
That's right. Nothing. Silence. Pouting. This worked pretty well over the years, until I got smart enough to realize what was happening. Once pouting was identified for what it was, a communication turn-off, it lost its effectiveness too.

We were finally honest about these roadblocks. But we still had a few more to tackle.

UNEXPRESSED EXPECTATIONS

Unexpressed expectations is another roadblock that cannot be ignored. These are the things we desire and hope for, perhaps even set as goals or see as needs, but that we fail to express. Many a child has failed because of unexpressed expectations at school and at home. Home-based businesses have been unsuccessful because of this, and so have marriages.

Unexpressed expectations can come in many forms. Because my original home-based business was the direct sale of Christian books, I witnessed a brand of unexpected expectations unique to a business/ministry. People began their business as a ministry, a good way to get great books into people's hands. Then they left the business because they weren't making any money. What? That doesn't make sense . . . get in for ministry and get out for lack of income? It *does* make sense in the light of unexpressed expectations. The unexpressed expectation was that income would be generated. If good business principles were not applied, that unexpressed expectation wasn't met and the business was dissolved.

ONE MORE ROADBLOCK

And, finally, the truth of the matter is that good communication takes effort and many times we are just plain lazy. If you doubt that laziness is actually a roadblock in our society, let's look at an interesting statistic. This particular survey that I'll be quoting has very little to do with evaluating communication skills but does have quite a bit to do with evaluating laziness.

According to *Health* magazine, "73% of Americans surveyed said that flossing was as important as brushing" while only "28% floss daily."[5] Hmmmmmmmm . . . a little discrepancy in the numbers.

We know that good communication is essential to the success of not only a home-based business, but a healthy marriage, and yet we are lazy. This roadblock, once recognized, is not difficult to conquer. It is essentially our choice. Many times, however, we say "I can't" when we actually mean "I choose not to." I once heard the words "I can't" taken through the following evolution: "I can't . . . I don't . . . I won't . . . I choose not to." For example, we might say, "I can't become a better listener." Is that true? No, it is our choice to become (or not become) better listeners. Or "I can't reveal my true agenda. Things will never get done!" No, again, it is our choice whether we disclose our agendas and develop better communication or whether we keep them hidden and risk poor communication. Don't be lazy. Choosing good communication can allow a couple to work together and to honestly evaluate the motivation of the home-based business as it changes and as daily lives change.

NOTES

1. Nicholas Boothman, *How to Make People Like You* (New York: Workman Publishing, 2000), 55.
2. Bob Rosner, "Become More Attentive with a Little Practice," *The Champaign-Urbana [IL] News-Gazette*, 19 December 2000, D-1.

3. Ibid.

4. Ibid.

5. "Vital Statistics," *Health*, September 1998, 20.

12

YOUR KEY RESPONSIBILITY:
HOMEMAKING

After you have taken the time to define your home-based business, it's time to describe your home-based-business responsibilities. Getting a grasp on these responsibilities will help you to further identify your time commitment. Although the responsibilities may vary somewhat from mom to mom, we'll examine the typical, universally accepted responsibilities of a home-based-business mom.

NO HOUSEWIFE

When I was in grade school, I was asked to complete paperwork each year that asked, among other things, these two questions: (1) What is your father's occupation? (2) What is your mother's occupation? My dad's was always easy—dentist. But I remember getting into big trouble one year when my mother saw that I had said her occupation was "housewife." I can still hear her words.

"I am not a housewife," she said indignantly. "I am not married to a house. I'm married to your dad, and I am a homemaker!" Her words made an impact on me. (Obviously! I can still remember them thirty-five years later.) Have you ever felt like a housewife when your desire was to be a homemaker?

A HOMEMAKER

What is a homemaker? What are the responsibilities of a home-maker? A homemaker is a home economist and family manager, an administrator, an overseer, a handyman, a treasurer, and much, much more. But beyond all these things, a homemaker creates a *home* for her family. She makes a dwelling place that is special . . . not because of its grandeur or its opulent furnishings, not because of "stuff," but because it's home. Home is a place of safety and warmth, of love and acceptance—a refuge. Home is a joyful and peaceful place of celebration—a retreat. And home provides a solid spiritual foundation—it is a rock. Thus a homemaker creates a dwelling place that is a refuge, a retreat, and a rock.

HOME AS A REFUGE

God is our refuge and strength, an ever-present help in trouble. Therefore we will not fear, though the earth give way and the mountains fall into the heart of the sea, though its waters roar and foam and the mountains quake with their surging. (Psalm 46:1–3)

A homemaker's responsibility includes providing a refuge for her family to mirror God's refuge for His children: a place of shelter, protection, and security. Even though the earth and mountains seem secure, they are not. The world can be a very troubling place. Battles are fought each day, and these battles are not fought only in the world of adults. Far too often a child's day includes put-downs, ridicule, and attacks from every side. Our children are belittled and criticized, embarrassed and deflated by their peers and unfortunately by adults as well. After a hard day at school or at work, it is good to know that *home* is waiting with welcoming arms.

A Really Bad Day

Jake had a rough day at school. Andrew, the class bully and the most physically mature boy in the fifth grade, had decided that Jake would be his target of the week. (Hopefully it would be for *just* one week.) Finally, one day, Jake reacted to being under attack and poked back at Andrew in retaliation after physical education class. Before Andrew could clean Jake's plow, Mrs. Murray stepped in and scolded Jake.

The day didn't get much better, either. In spelling, Mrs. Murray put the class into teams for review. Jake's mistake cost his team the prize. That wasn't popular.

Jake's mom had packed a PB and J sandwich for lunch, and he managed to slop the J on his T-shirt. Then it was time for recess, but Jake couldn't find the math worksheet he had completed the night before, so he was required to stay inside and finish another one. And just when Jake thought that it couldn't get any worse, his pen broke and leaked ink all over his new jeans.

This, my friend, was a bad day for Jake. The best thing that could happen at this point was that Jake got home to his refuge, where he was safe and accepted.

Creating a Refuge

So, if making our home a refuge is a part of our responsibility as a home-based-business mom, how can we do it? What can make our family feel safe and warm, loved and accepted?

Creating a safe refuge doesn't necessarily mean we literally have bolts and locks on our doors to keep out danger. Instead, as homemakers we want to ensure that, within our four walls, our family feels safe from things like ridicule and abuse. That is the kind of safety Jake (the boy with the terrible day) desperately needed. I am not so naive as to believe that this kind of refuge is offered in every home. But I am not addressing every home. I am talking to you . . . the home-based-business mom who desires to walk that tightrope to her goals of honoring God and her family as she pursues a home-based business. You and I both have the desire to create a refuge for our families.

One aspect that is important in a refuge is for those who come there to feel respected. Teaching children to respect one another is not an easy job. Sibling rivalry can prove to be a stress in a family, making a home feel less than safe.

A homemaker can do many things to promote harmony in the home. If Mom and Dad show respect to each other and to their children (with their words and with their actions), the chances are greatly increased that the children will follow suit.

Many times after a meal my husband says "thank you" to me, the preparer. As a result, my children are prone to do the same. And no one ever leaves Grandma's house after a meal without a big "thank you." It's modeling and training.

With our sons, we wanted to take special care so that they would grow to appreciate one another. The word *grow* in that sentence is significant. We didn't expect our children to be best friends from the day son number two was born. That would have been unreasonable. What we did do was encourage them to capitalize on their individual strengths, eliminate rivalry as much as possible, and help them to allow for one another's differences and faults and to identify and applaud each other's victories and good decisions.

Creature Comforts

A refuge has certain creature comforts that are soothing and that help to make us feel loved and protected. Again, it's not necessarily the "stuff"; it's the feeling that is in a place.

For many of us, a refuge contains some particular food or foods. Do people actually have Christmas without date nut pudding? Can anything top Grandma Ruthie's rib roast? With the plethora of eating disorders in our nation today, I certainly don't want to suggest that food is a necessary way to say "I love you" or that your refuge must be stocked with an overabundance of goodies in order to be effective. That is not true. Nevertheless, the occasional cooking of a favorite dish can remind someone by sight, taste, and smell how special he is.

The sense of smell, by the way, is a powerful thing that can enhance our place of refuge. When I was a young girl, my mother made homemade bread nearly every week. She always timed its completion with my arrival home from school. Even today, when I wake up to the smell of bread in our bread machine, I think of my mom and the nurturing she accomplished with a few cups of flour and a little yeast.

I can also remember the smell of my great aunt's home. Aunt Bert, the closest thing I had to a grandmother, was a wonderful maiden lady who went out of her way to love and encourage her many nieces and nephews. Her home smelled like furniture polish, old books, and her favorite talcum powder. Remembering those smells brings me warm memories of a place of refuge.

What are some comforting smells you can remember? Maybe it's your mom's perfume or your dad's aftershave. Maybe it's the smell of your favorite dish being made with loving hands. Perhaps your refuge contained the smell of a fire in the fireplace or of hamburgers on the grill. Just as certain smells elicit warm feelings and memories of your refuge, you can be responsible for those as a homemaker who is establishing a refuge for her family.

Maybe you have difficulty equating your childhood home with a refuge. Even if that is the case, you can still choose to build a refuge for your own family as a home-based-business mom. Remember that God is your refuge and He will supernaturally protect you, shelter you, and provide you with security. Nothing can rob you of His protection. And, in turn, He will enable you to create for your own family the earthly refuge you may have never experienced. Assuming the homemaker's responsibility of creating a refuge takes a commitment of time and energy.

HOME AS A RETREAT

Splendor and majesty are before him; strength and joy in his dwelling place.
(1 Chronicles 16:27)

The word *retreat* has some overlap with the word *refuge*. It can symbolize a place apart. But for me, a retreat also conjures up thoughts of joy, peace, and celebration. Perhaps that is due to the fact that I have had the privilege of attending some absolutely glorious ladies' retreats. And I am convinced that a homemaker can provide a dwelling place that resonates with joy and peace.

Years ago I had the opportunity to speak at a weekend seminar for home-based-business moms. After the first session, which was geared to getting folks to relax and to start to enjoy themselves, we took a short break. As the ladies congregated for coffee and conversation, a kind woman approached me to say how delightful our first session had been. "I laughed and laughed. It was wonderful!" she said, still beaming and trying to catch her breath. Then suddenly she stopped and added quite solemnly, "We don't laugh much at our house."

Wow! I really felt sorry for her and for the people at her house. Her statement was distressing. There could have been a number of causes for the gloom, none of which were necessarily the woman's fault. But my hope was that perhaps now she would begin to look for ways to bring joy and laughter into her home.

You don't have to be a natural-born comedian to bring joy into your home. Actually, it's more of an attitude—an attitude of celebration. We have so many things to celebrate: life, love, Christ, family, the list goes on and on. Celebration is the essence of making your home a retreat.

With a little imagination, you can discover many things to celebrate. In fact, if you are imagination-impaired, you can even purchase a calendar that lists every wild and crazy (and I guess "official") holiday on record. (Haven't you always wanted to celebrate national knee sock day?)

Celebrating Christmas

Your celebrations do not have to be elaborate, but some obvious holidays call for a certain standard of fussing. Undoubtedly, Christmas is the first one most of us think of. Now that's a holiday that can easily get out of hand with the focus on everything but Jesus—the reason for the season. It is easy to forget what we are celebrating and to actually be much too exhausted to celebrate anyway. So what can we do? One suggestion is to include your family in the preparation. The season of Advent is a time of making ready, preparing for the coming of Christ. Perhaps your kids can anticipate the celebration of Christ's birthday more completely if they help in the preparation. Now, before you get out your list of Christmas jobs and start divvying them up, let me suggest a way to elicit help that can be more fun and effective, especially with younger children.

When my sons were little I created a very personalized Advent calendar. I found a banner with twenty-five pockets to be filled on each day of December until Christmas. But rather than put a tiny toy or some candy into the pockets, I wrote a poem for each day that indicated what Christmas preparation/activity we would enjoy that day. Believe me, I am no Elizabeth Barrett Browning. I just had a very easy poem-writing process.

First I made a list of the Christmas jobs (sending cards, baking cookies, cleaning house for the party, buying the tree, decorating the tree, hanging the outdoor lights, etc.) and all the Christmas activities (caroling, shopping, Sunday school program, watching the Charlie Brown Christmas television special, etc.). Then it was a matter of deciding the day for each event. The poems were simple two-line jingles. The key to writing them was to end the first line with an easy-to-rhyme word and to keep the number of syllables the same in both lines. (And guess what? Your kids don't really care about either of these things anyway.)

> "Today we'll buy the Christmas tree.
> It will be fun for you and me."

> "Please give the envelopes a lick.
> You do it right and they will stick."

Something as uncomplicated as these Advent poems made the preparation fun and exciting. Christmas day was our focus, but the journey to that day was filled with celebration too. (And obviously,

Mom was getting some much needed help.) This simple idea can make each day of Advent a celebration of the coming Christ.

Theme Parties

It is easy to think of celebration ideas if you think in terms of a theme. Some are obvious, like Valentine's Day. That's the perfect time to make heart-shaped pancakes. On Saint Patrick's Day I have been treated to green milk (lots of food coloring with a rather disgusting result). July 4 is synonymous with independence fireworks. And on and on.

Think up a theme and you can celebrate less apparent things too. We once had a pig party that was actually a little elaborate. Everyone wore pink, and dinner was slop (goulash), pink punch, and dessert. Now there's a theme!

You can celebrate the first day of school with a breakfast or lunch stop at a fast food restaurant and start a tradition. You can celebrate the last day of school with a family bike ride and picnic lunch.

What about Tuesday being library day? That is something you can celebrate each week. The children's library is a wonderful place to spend a little time, and it encourages your children to celebrate the gift of good books and of reading.

Adjusting to Change

Obviously, the celebrations must change as your family dynamics change. No longer do I take my boys to the library on Tuesday. (Two of them are in college and spend much more time there than one half hour a week . . . I hope.) But birthdays are still a time of celebration. In our family a person may not be honored on the actual day of his birth, but we *will* celebrate his special day. And at each person's birthday celebration, the guest of honor selects the dinner menu.

Easter is celebrated at Grandma Jean's house with an Easter egg hunt, even though some of the hunters are now twenty-something. That egg hunt celebration will probably continue with its original cast of characters until our children and/or their cousins have their own children who want their fair share of the chocolate eggs.

Daily Celebrations

What is dinnertime like at your house? Is it a time of visiting and celebrating the day, or is it a necessary chow break to sustain life? If you are like the typical United States family, the chances are great you are unfamiliar with the traditional dinnertime your grandmother hosted each day. Maybe you could consider reviving this old-fashioned family celebration to some degree. Perhaps a Sunday dinner is possible. Or maybe Friday night is doable with a little effort. I would encourage you to try. It will undoubtedly (even if not immediately) be worth your effort.

All these ideas can stimulate your own thinking and can even be adapted to contribute to your home's becoming a place of joy, peace, and celebration—a place of retreat.

HOME AS A ROCK

Therefore everyone who hears these words of mine and puts them into practice is like a wise man who built his house on the rock. The rain came down, the streams rose, and the winds blew and beat against that house, yet it did not fall, because it had its foundation on the rock. (Matthew 7:24–25)

As a homemaker, one of our responsibilities and opportunities is to make our home a rock. Just as in the Scripture quoted above, we want our home to be unshakable even when the storms of life crash around us.

The *only* way that is possible is to construct that home on the proper foundation, the foundation of Jesus Christ. How do we make our home a rock? I believe it is a twofold process. It is based both on what we say and what we do.

Earlier, in the chapter on good communication, we discussed the importance of congruent verbal and nonverbal communication. When we say one thing and do another, our words are not believed. Our actions truly do speak louder than our words. Adults sometimes classify the discrepancy between one's words and actions as hypocrisy. Kids just know that things don't line up. "Do what I say and not what I do" is a terrible adage! It is one that acts to shatter the rock of foundation.

The Vow on the Machine Shed

Years ago, when our older sons were two and four, my husband began a project. With an enlarged pattern, a jigsaw, and sheet of plywood, he created an identifying sign for our machine shed. Then, between sunrise service and Sunday school on Easter morning, he climbed the extension ladder and attached the sign to the front of the shed. Since that time, "Jesus is Lord" has greeted each passerby and everyone who has turned into our lane.

As the boys grew up, they not only saw that sign each day, but they witnessed their dad living those words to the best of his ability. Because of that consistency, our shed sign helped our home to be a rock. If John had attached those words and then failed to honor them in his own life, they would have been meaningless or perhaps even detrimental to our children.

On the Air

On more than one occasion while my oldest son was in college, he and I were asked to be guests on a radio show called "Sports Saturday." The station that broadcast the show also airs my daily radio show, "Live Life Intentionally," and we have a great time working together. The host of "Sports Saturday" was one of the area television sportscasters, and each Saturday he spent one hour bringing people up-to-date on collegiate and national sports information while highlighting various Christian athletes and coaches. My son Matthew was on the University of Illinois football team for two seasons and then served for five semesters as a student coach. That's why he was a guest.

Annnnnnnnnd, you're thinking, *why were you on the show?*

I was not invited to do the show because I am a big-time athlete or coach. No, in this particular case, my claim to fame was being on the State Board for the Illinois Fellowship of Christian Athletes. The Illinois FCA sponsored the show. And Ron, the host, felt the combination of Matthew and Mom brought an interesting perspective to "Sports Saturday."

The format for the show is very relaxed. There are no scripts, just a loose roadmap of where the conversation will go. As we were wrapping up a show we did before the last home game of the University of Illinois football season, Ron asked Matthew an interesting question. The question and the answer were recorded for posterity.

"Matthew," Ron began, "what about Kendra the author and speaker . . . You know her as the mom. You've seen her from a different perspective. What's your thought on that?" (In other words, "What is she *really* like?")

I listened intently, wondering how my twenty-two-year-old would address that question—and how I would feel when he was finished.

"The funny thing is," he began, "they are the same person. If you go to hear my mom speak, or read her books, that's how she is at home. She's upbeat at home. She lives the things that are in her books. And that's what's nice for me. There's a sense of pride and a good feeling knowing that Mom isn't writing these things to sell books or because *you* should do this (but I certainly don't). The things you see when you see her speak or if you listen to her on the radio or read her books, that's exactly how she is when she's making pancakes in the morning at home. That's real nice for all three of us kids."

Needless to say, I was smiling on the inside and on the outside and was so pleased that we had captured those words on tape! But let me continue to transcribe the dialogue and you will see that I definitely had *not* scripted my son.

"Oh, is she a good cook?" Ron asked (obviously in reference to Matthew's parting words about the pancakes).

His reply? "Dad's a very good cook!"

Ahhhhhhh, humbled in the nick of time! But what I had been privileged enough to hear up to that point was the unrehearsed testimonial from one of my children that my talk and my walk had distinct similarities. And that is one of the aspects of the home-based-business mom's responsibility . . . to make her home a rock.

Being a homemaker and creating a home that is a refuge, a retreat, and a rock is a portion of the description of a home-based-business mom's responsibilities; and it is definitely a portion of the time commitment.

13

YOUR RECURRING RESPONSIBILITY:
HOUSEKEEPING

Another aspect of your home-based-business responsibilities that will demand a time commitment is housekeeping. This involves the tasks of maintaining a household. Almost all of these responsibilities could be done by someone you have hired for the job. That is in sharp contrast to homemaking, which is a labor of love.

Even though housekeeping tasks can be hired out, the average home-based-business mom may not have the monetary resources to do that exclusively. Perhaps the home-based-business mom has some-one help her clean her house, but cleaning is only one aspect. For our purposes I've divided housekeeping into three categories: cooking, cleaning, and laundry. Entire books have been written to address each of these categories and give helpful hints about how each can be done more effectively and more efficiently. I have listed some of these resources at the conclusion of this chapter. But let's take a broad look at each category.

THE RESPONSIBILITY OF COOKING

The Proverbs 31 do-it-all gal "gets up while it is still dark; she provides food for her family and portions for her servant girls" (v. 15). There is no way around it—cooking for your family is a definite time commitment. If you do not employ a cook or eat out the majority of the time, you must develop a plan to make this responsibility as enjoyable and efficient as possible.

I finally realized that the biggest hang-up I have with cooking is the time involved. Because of that I have spent years looking for ways to save time.

One important time-saver involves shopping. Because of our rural location, seven miles from the grocery store, I try to shop only once a week. This plan saves me time, and it will save you time and typically save you money too. How often do you stop at the grocery store for one or two necessary items and walk out of the store with four full bags of groceries? A single trip cuts down on impulse buying.

Planning menus for the entire week (something I'm still working on) is also a shopping time-saver. You can read the ads and plan your menus around the specials for that week. Even if you have mastered the art of organized, infrequent grocery shopping, you can still find other ways to save time in meal preparation.

Big Batches = Big Time-Savers

The greatest time-saving system I ever discovered was the idea of cooking ahead and freezing. I am writing this just two weeks after Christmas. My mother-in-law fed anywhere from six to twenty people every day for a week. In spite of this amazing feat, she was relaxed, pleasant, and organized throughout the marathon.

Undoubtedly, many factors contributed to her ability to truly be "the hostess with the mostest," but the primary one was her ability and choice to do as much food preparation as possible weeks before the guests arrived. She has discovered recipes that taste great and freeze well, and she has capitalized on this knowledge.

Once-a-Month Cooking, by Mimi Wilson and Mary Beth Lagerborg, and *The 30-Day Gourmet*, by Nanci Slagle and Tara Wohlenhaus, both operate under the same premise as my mother-in-law, Jean—making food ahead and freezing it. When I first took the challenge of marathon cooking, I learned that it was imperative to actually follow the instructions in the text. For example, I failed to take seriously the recommendation not "to do any extra baking on the days you're doing this method."[1] Actually, I tried to do extra *everything*, from childcare to husband help. As a result I found myself in tears shortly after noon, proclaiming, "I'll never get finished. I'll still be cooking next Tuesday!" Pay attention to the experts. They know what they are talking about!

The second time I tried making thirty entrées in one day, I cooked with a girlfriend. We may not have been any more efficient, but the process was definitely more fun. Next, three of us tried cooking at the church. That was more efficient because of the increased counter space and the multiple burners and ovens.

Momma Be Cookin' Club

As the word got out about our adventure in cooking multiple entrées in one day, we had more and more women who were interested. Instead of meeting for a marathon cooking day, we tried another approach.

We established the Momma Be Cookin' Club. Each club member made one particular entrée recipe multiplied by the number of club members. These were frozen in disposable containers, and the cost of each entrée plus container was calculated. Once each month we met to exchange entrées and settle up financially.

This was a fun answer to more efficient cooking. It is much easier to make ten pans of lasagna than to make ten different entrées. The Momma Be Cookin' Club was an answer for many months.

The Daily Job

On a daily basis, cooking more efficiently can be greatly enhanced by simply planning ahead. My goal is to defrost the necessary ingredients the night before they are to be used. That really beats zapping a frozen chunk of meat at five P.M. (or ordering pizza).

If I am home during the day (one of the joys of being a home-based-business mom), I can accomplish some dinner preparation as I cook, serve, or clean up breakfast or lunch. That's another example of planning ahead.

My husband is a pretty good cook. His mother went back to college when he was in sixth grade, and he learned to follow her directions and to master some of the basics of food preparation. When we were first married, he had much more experience in the kitchen than I had. In spite of that, ultimately the kitchen became my domain. That is typical. I am very thankful, however, that because of John's culinary experience, I am not required to cook ahead when I will be gone at a speaking engagement. John is capable and he is willing. Nevertheless, the cooking responsibilities and time commitment are essentially mine.

THE RESPONSIBILITY OF CLEANING

A friend of mine said that, if her home-based business earned no more than enough to pay for someone to clean her house, it was a great trade-off. I understand that statement. There is no reference to cleaning in conjunction with our Proverbs 31 do-it-all gal. Maybe she felt the same way my friend did and handled the task of cleaning the same way.

One of the most helpful hints I ever learned in regard to cleaning was this: Identify the expectations of your family (especially your spouse). This principle actually applies to all aspects of housekeeping. For example, my husband is much more concerned about the time a meal is served than he is about the menu. He enjoys eating on time. Also, my children are not impressed by "presentation" when it comes to dining. Their biggest interest is quantity.

In cleaning, as in every other scenario, expectations cannot be guessed or surmised. It is important to do a little research and ask about those expectations.

Expectations when it comes to cleaning . . . even as I write those words I can imagine two people with incredibly different cleaning expectations. One of them considers a supply of Q-tip swabs essential for adequate cleaning (you know, to get into the crevices around the controls on your stove top). And the other is a piler who quickly scoops up the piles before company comes. There are no Q-tips in her cleaning supplies . . . maybe just a large shovel. Both houses are sanitary and welcoming, yet they are at either end of the cleaning continuum. I have typically occupied a spot somewhere between these two extremes, chosen because of my family's identified expectations.

Much to my delight, I discovered early in our marriage that my husband did not have immaculate expectations for my cleaning. (Send back the Q-tips!) He liked things neat, but he realized that with young children perfection was not an option. John doesn't notice two-day-old dust or even care about it. He does, however, want the family room to be negotiable even in the dark.

I am 5'5" and my husband is 5'10". Neither one of us can actually see the top of the refrigerator. Do you understand what I'm saying? Neither one of us can see it. Neither one of us really cares whether or not it is covered with dust. If, by chance, someone over six feet tall comes for a visit in our home *and* I think the person might be anti-dust, I simply keep him out of the kitchen.

Again, there are many books that can help you with the task of cleaning. *The Messies Motivator* by Sandra Felton is a great resource. So are assorted books by Don Aslett, the king of cleaning.

The Early Years

My children were a big help to me when they were younger. Everyone had his cleaning assignment for the week, and it was expected that those assignments would be completed before we played on Saturday. For better or worse, I was raised with the idea that work came before play, and so I carried that tradition to the next generation.

I learned early on that a written list of tasks was much better than me verbalizing each new task as the last one was finished. One advantage to the list was that the boys knew there would be closure on their jobs. This helped speed up their work. A never-ending list tended to do just the opposite and produce a work slowdown.

As the boys got older, they were involved in many school activities that claimed much of their free time. That, combined with chores on the farm, took them off my cleaning staff. Nevertheless, they received early training and experience that will benefit them in later years.

Just Do It

One of the difficult things I have discovered about cleaning is the idea of "do it now." In years past, I used to hope that by ignoring certain unpleasant tasks they would miraculously disappear. They didn't. When we do a job right away (i.e., washing the dishes or removing a spot), the chore is almost always easier than it will be later if it is postponed.

THE RESPONSIBILITY OF LAUNDRY

My final category in housekeeping responsibilities is laundry. The Proverbs 31 woman seems to be quite a seamstress (vv. 13, 22, 24), but the Bible does not specifically mention who washed all those clothes. I once heard someone refer to modern appliances as "servant girls." That gave an interesting twist. It helped me to appreciate the wonderful conveniences these machines supply, just as I would appreciate the help of another person.

Laundry is an amazing task. Claiming total victory in the laundry room is very difficult. I have threatened to force everyone to remain in the same clothes for multiple days so that I could conquer the laundry for once, but I've never made good on that threat.

My goal with the laundry is to provide clean clothes for my family in an efficient, effective manner. Laundry, cooking, and even cleaning take on very different looks depending on the number of people in your family. When my eldest went to college, I discovered that he was responsible for more than one-fifth of the laundry even though he was one-fifth of the family. My number of loads of laundry shrank and then shrank again when my second son went to college.

Regardless of how many loads a week you average, having a plan always makes it more efficient. At one point when the boys were young, I had two laundry baskets, one dark and one light, and it was the kids' responsibility to sort their laundry as they pitched it into the baskets.

The Bath-Towel Dilemma

In my extensive laundry research (please smile here) I have discovered that the majority of moms are overloaded with laundering bath towels. All of you who are burdened by this, please take note . . . there is no scientific proof that your child will contract a serious disease from actually reusing a bath towel. Do not believe what your child has been telling you! Most of the time those towels are thrown into the dirty clothes basket because they are still slightly damp. (That's what happens when they're left in a wad on the floor.) And worse than the dampness is the thought that the damp towel was made damp by drying *someone else*. ("Oh gross! I might have to dry with a towel my brother used!")

One simple answer to the dilemma of extensive towel washing is to assign a specific towel color to each person in the family. The instructions are that your towel, designated by a specific color, is to be used for X number of days, at which time Mom will wash it. If you don't like damp towels, hang yours up! And don't use someone else's.

Your laundry and the life of your washer and dryer will benefit from this simple idea.

Play Ball!

Sports uniforms can be a real laundry challenge. The rule? Put them in the laundry room when you come home from the sporting event if you want them clean by the next one. Make sure your kids have plenty of socks and underwear. It is cheaper to buy another half-dozen pairs of underwear than it is to run your washer to keep junior in undies.

I like to throw a load of dirty clothes into the washer in the early evening and then start the dryer before I go to bed. Then in the morning I have a clean batch of wash to fold.

HOUSEKEEPING VS. HOMEMAKING

All of these housekeeping tasks—cooking, cleaning, and laundry—are very necessary and must be counted in on our time commitment to meeting our family's needs. They all have a part in defining our home-based-business responsibilities. They are not, however, the essence of homemaking.

While I was at a speaking engagement in a very affluent community, the principal of a private school in the area told me a story. One family who sent their daughter to his school was very wealthy. They had a big beautiful home complete with two wings of bedrooms. Undoubtedly the housekeeping chores were all done to perfection by people who had been hired by the family.

The family itself consisted of a mom, a dad, and this one teenage daughter. Each night the parents slept in one wing of the house and the daughter slept in the other wing. Unfortunately, it would seem that the house, with impeccable housekeeping, was not a home. For the daughter had told her principal (who then told me) that each night after everyone was in bed, she took her pillow and slept outside her parents' bedroom door.

Where was the home? The refuge? The retreat? The rock? In this case, it was nonexistent. Keeping house without making a home is incredibly inadequate for a family. Both of these responsibilities are aspects of our time commitment.

RESOURCES

Don Aslett, *Make Your House Do the Housework*, rev. ed. (Cincinnati, Ohio: Betterway, 1995).

————. *No Time to Clean* (Pocatello, Idaho: Marsh Creek, 2000).

Sandra Felton, *The Messies Motivator* (Grand Rapids: Revell, 1986).

Nanci Slagle and Tara Wohlenhaus, *The 30-Day Gourmet* (Brownsburg, Ind.: 30-Day Gourmet, 1995).

Taste of Home's Quick Cooking, 5400 S. 60th St., Greendale, WI 53121; (800) 344-6913

Mimi Wilson and Mary Beth Lagerborg, *Once-a-Month Cooking* (Colorado Springs: Focus on the Family, 1991).

NOTE

1. Mimi Wilson and Mary Beth Lagerborg, *Once-a-Month Cooking* (Colorado Springs: Focus on the Family, 1991), 10.

14

THE MOTIVATION FOR YOUR RESPONSIBILITY:
FAMILY

We have already discussed the importance of priorities and family, with husband and children ranking numbers two and three respectively. We have also mentioned that ranking does not indicate time allotment. But a family does take time, and we will need to describe the family responsibilities not addressed earlier in order to determine our time commitment.

A RELATIONSHIP WITH YOUR HUSBAND

In addition to the home-based business responsibilities we have already covered, building and maintaining a vital relationship with your husband takes time. If you want to have your husband support and encourage you in your home-based business, it requires good communication, a little home cooking, clean laundry, and more.

Relationships are nurtured by spending time together. That time commitment can take various forms.

When I first began my home-based business, I tried to be very frugal in every area. The timing of my phone calls was one way I could save some money. My home-based business began when no phone plans gave free nights and weekends, but the billing system did give reduced rates after 5:00 P.M. and on the weekends. So of course I tried to schedule my calls after five, thinking this was the wisest decision.

At the time I began my home-based business, John was teaching school and coaching. He came home every day around 5:30, and what did he discover? He found his boys playing and his wife giving her full attention to some stranger on the other end of the telephone wire.

I thought I was being wise and saving a little money. In truth, I was being foolish because my husband wanted me to spend time with him when he arrived home after work. Finally, after several confrontations, I adjusted my schedule, spent a few extra cents per call, and prepared for John's arrival home so that I could give him my full attention. Attention . . . that is an essential part of the responsibilities of a home-based-business mom.

TRAVEL AND A FAMILY PERSPECTIVE

As time went on and my home-based business began to include traveling, I learned another valuable lesson. Off I would go for an overnight away—maybe to a business conference for my home-based business or in later years to speak at a ladies' retreat. I would give my all for the one or two days I was gone. I would burn the candle at both ends and not pass up one opportunity to learn or to speak.

Do I need to tell you that, by the time I returned to the comfort of my own home, I was exhausted? I would open the door at home and greet my dear family, including my sweet husband who had played the role of Mr. Mom all weekend. After a quick smile, I would crash on the couch. My exhaustion did not bring out the best in me. My comatose state did not lend itself to answering questions like

"How was the conference?" Nor did it allow me to express appreciation for all the tasks John had accomplished as caretaker of the house and single parent of the kids in my absence. The result was typically one very overworked, overlooked hubby and one very exhausted, self-centered wife.

The answer? I've always said that defining the problem brings you more than halfway to the solution. Once I realized what was happening, I made a concerted effort to reserve a portion of my energy for re-entry into the family. Many times I scheduled a restful day following a big trip, anticipating my weariness. With some energy in reserve I was able to extend love and appreciation to John and also to share with him some of the excitement of the conference. Both of these things helped to keep us "singing from the same song sheet," and they made him more receptive to the idea of assuming the Mr. Mom role again.

GETTING AWAY WITH YOUR HUSBAND

I am sure that many of you have heard of the advantages of having a "date night" with your spouse. We have never scheduled that type of time together, probably because after John stopped teaching school and went to a more flexible schedule, we had many opportunities for a quiet lunch together at home.

One scheduled time that we *did* appreciate, however, was what we fondly referred to as our honeymoon. Each year, near the date of our anniversary, we made arrangements for the children and went away together for at least twenty-four hours. This respite from everyday life with its stresses and pressures provided a great boost for our marriage. The purpose was romance, and we made no bones about it. We weren't combining it with business or childcare or any other "duty." It was a time to focus on each other, reflect on the past year, and dream about the next.

Taking time to be with your husband is crucial. If you are a Type A person like me, always busy and always planning, sometimes the idea of sitting beside your husband on the couch and watching a movie (without an additional task at hand) can be a little unnerving.

But for me it is something John enjoys. Whenever I have the urge to feel I'm "wasting time," I remind myself how nice it is that he *wants* me by his side (and how comfortable it is there!). A home-based-business mom must make a time commitment to be at her husband's side (wide awake and without her laptop).

In his book *His Needs, Her Needs,* Dr. Willard Harley developed a list of the top five needs for each gender. He suggested that a husband's number two need is "recreational companionship."

> It is not uncommon for women, when they are single, to join men in pursuing their interests. They find themselves hunting, fishing, playing football, and watching movies they would never have chosen on their own. After marriage wives often try to interest their husbands in activities more to their own liking. If their attempts fail, they may encourage their husbands to continue their recreational activities without them. [1]

Being available for recreation and just for being together is an important aspect of meeting your husband's needs.

MAKING TIME FOR CHILDREN'S TIME DEMANDS

Have you ever noticed that your kids require a big time commitment? I've occasionally observed adults who seem to be totally uninterested in their children—who never attend a ballgame or an honors night or a school play. When I see that, I have to wonder why they bothered to have children in the first place. Who has time?

The time demands of children change as the children and their interests and activities change. In regard to activities, I am not an advocate of kids' untempered "joining." In our home, the basic plan of attack was that schoolwork came first, nothing preempted church, and other activities could be added if they fit into the family schedule. A student who is involved in extracurricular activities has several things going for him: (1) The student usually must maintain certain academic standards to continue involvement. (2) A busy teenager (do not read *swamped* teenager) has fewer unsupervised hours and fewer opportunities to engage in inappropriate activities. (3) Extracurriculars help kids develop social skills and they can be character-building.

When your child sings or wrestles or performs or competes, your support of the event gives the two of you another thing in common. Please do not misinterpret what I'm saying. I do not believe kids should be pushed into activities or overbooked to the point of fatigue or stress. And I do not believe a parent must sacrifice all to be in attendance at *every* event including her child. Occasionally important things may have to preempt your child's event. This will simply remind him that the world, indeed, does not revolve around him (a misconception of many youth). If you find yourself missing a great number of your child's activities, however, honestly evaluate if your children are still maintaining their high position on your list of priorities.

I believe that academic performance is important and that children should be encouraged to do their best for the very joy of doing one's best (and because it is a good habit to get into and has great rewards). Starting at an early age to encourage your children to set God-honoring priorities is a wonderful idea!

Summer League

Our youngest son, Jonathan, loves sports. One summer he was asked to play on a traveling basketball team with some very good athletes. The practice was during the week and the games were on several weekends—all over the state of Illinois. We told Jonathan that he could accept the invitation, but that he would have to let the coach know that he would be attending church every week.

That was fine with all involved. The commitment to the corporate worship of God each week was not too difficult to achieve. Usually John and I simply located a church in the town in which he was playing and checked the service schedule. Then we made sure we took advantage of the opportunity to worship. Basketball didn't come before church. Maybe only one time did Jonathan have to miss one of the games because it was scheduled at precisely the same time as every church in town.

The only complication came one weekend when neither John nor I could go to a tournament. We didn't feel as if we could ask another adult who would already be attending to assume our responsibility. Finally a plan developed. Matthew, our oldest son and a licensed driver, went with Jonathan. He drove him to Macomb, Illinois, on the other side of the state, watched him play basketball on Saturday, stayed with him in the hotel on Saturday night, went to church with him on Sunday, and then watched more ballgames that afternoon. Thank goodness Matthew likes basketball (and Jonathan).

Quality Time vs. Quantity Time

The debate over quality versus quantity time has existed for a generation now. There are strong opinions on both sides. My basic premise is this: Quality time is what occasionally happens while you're busy having quantity time. When a mom feels the pressure to make each moment with her child one of quality, it is ridiculously stressful.

That is the beauty of a home-based business. While I sat at my desk, my preschoolers sat at theirs. I had pencils and markers and paper, and so did they. When I unpacked books, they helped. They learned to treat the books gently and with respect. And because my home-based business was the direct sale of Christian books, they read and I read to them. After all, we were working!

When there was a conference with family invited, we all went. The boys heard excellent speakers in their children's programs and saw interesting places around the country. As they got older, they became facilitators of the programs for younger children. And it all happened because their mom was a home-based-business mom.

Help!

I was speaking at a very large conference in Chicago several years ago, which was really the same conference given three times. I repeated the same message six times . . . two times on the first day followed by a two-day break, then two more times, another two-day break, and finally two more times. After the first day, I realized that

I needed help. The sessions were much bigger than the company had predicted, and there was no help for me at my book table. I called home that night in desperation. Could anyone drive to Chicago and help me?

My son Aaron, then just sixteen years old, was able to come to the rescue. After a quick lesson on processing a credit card and instruction of general book-table etiquette, he went to work. I wish he could have traveled with me everywhere! Not only did he rescue his mother, but he charmed the attendees at the conference with his dimples and his confidence. This experience was possible because of my home-based business.

All three of my sons have helped me with my radio show, and not just by supplying me with funny stories to tell. My oldest son, Matthew, has taken this responsibility for more than a year. Once when I was telling someone at the radio station what a great help he was to me, he smiled, rolled his eyes, and said from behind a cupped hand, "Mom just likes to see me once a month when she records her show."

OK, so he's a great help *and* fun to see? Seriously, all the boys have timed me at recording sessions, edited, corrected, and polished my shows. They have had very educational, very entertaining experiences because of my home-based business. It has expanded their horizons and given them poise. These are all benefits of the time commitment I made as a home-based-business mom.

One-on-One Opportunities

One of the time commitments to consider as a home-based-business mom is taking the opportunity to spend time with each child, one-on-one. Those of you who are parenting an only child have got this assignment wrapped up! But if you have more than one child in your family, you will have to be more creative to meet this goal. Again, my home-based business provided opportunities upon which I could capitalize. Maybe you haven't decided yet whether this is the route for you. Several occasions reaffirmed to me that this was the best thing for my family. For example, in their senior year of high school, both of my college-age sons went with me as I worked as a facilitator for CLASS (Christian Leaders, Authors, and Speakers Seminar).

When Matthew was a senior I enrolled him in the CLASSeminar, and we traveled together to Maryland. He gained a tremendous amount of skill, encouragement, and confidence in the area of speaking. And I gained three days alone with one of my favorite people. Aaron and I did the same thing two years later, traveling to New Orleans. The trips provided great learning and great memories. These were made possible because of my home-based business. It will be Jonathan's turn before too long.

When Aaron was in high school, he was on the Student Advisory Council for the Illinois State Board of Education. This group met occasionally during the school year, and I was able to accompany him to a Chicago meeting. We traveled from Champaign, Illinois, to downtown Chicago by train and enjoyed a fun day together. Then the next morning, I flew out of Chicago to a speaking engagement and he went to his meetings. What fun! What memories—all made possible because of my home-based business.

Jonathan, our youngest child, is now the only one at home. Life, for the most part, *finally* revolves around him, and we have had many opportunities to spend time together.

The first time both older sons were home from college after Jonathan had been an "only" for a few months, we were all having dinner together. "Well, Jonathan," said Matthew, talking as though the boys were alone, "how is it? Just you and the folks . . . all alone."

"Actually," Jonathan replied, "it's not too bad. The only hard thing is that I'm the only one here to entertain Mom."

There was some truth there! Poor boy.

Time together . . . it's part of our commitment to our children. Those of you with younger children may feel overwhelmed right now with the daily (and often unappreciated) time demands of your children. Take heart. For you too, the word "Mom" can shift from job description to term of endearment.

TAKING TIME OFF

In the state of Illinois, public schools are dismissed for Casmir Pulaski Day. It is one of the more obscure (though genuinely appreciated) holidays. One year I announced to my family that Casmir Pulaski Day was next week and that I intended to take the day off too. My boys' reaction was priceless. "How can you take a day off? You don't work!"

I actually did not find this proclamation distressing or offensive. They weren't referring to my "motherhood tasks." They knew they had meals and clean clothes. Instead, their question reflected their belief that I did not work because I was always available. They obviously did not feel slighted by my home-based business. I worked, but they didn't notice. They were still an outranking priority.

As a home-based-business mom, I was around. I was able to be the room mother, the show choir bus chaperone, and the van driver to FCA game day. I realize that moms who have chosen to work outside the home can also take time off work and volunteer for those kid-centered time commitments. As a home-based-business mom, however, I didn't have to get anyone's permission (except maybe my kids')—my schedule was my own.

NOTE

1. Willard F. Harley Jr., *His Needs, Her Needs* (Grand Rapids: Revell, 1986, 1994), 77.

15

TAKING TIME FOR A RELATIONSHIP WITH YOUR SAVIOR

So far you have defined your home-based business and described your home-based-business responsibilities, and now it is time to delight in your home-based faith. We have been working our way up the list of priorities, through four, three, and two; and now it is time to examine the time commitment to the number one priority—the Lord. I actually feel uncomfortable using the term *commitment*. In my mind that word equates with duty, discipline, and responsibility. Our time spent with the Lord is indeed a discipline, but it is so much more.

When I devote time to my home-based business, I potentially move toward my goals of reaching others for Christ through the written and spoken word. When I commit time to my children and to my husband, I potentially nurture and strengthen our relationships. All of these results are positive and worthy of a commitment of time. But the time I devote to enhancing my relationship with the Lord, when I make a time commitment to Him, has rewards that are beyond compare. It is truly a delight!

A GUARANTEE

The time commitment I make to priorities two through five—my husband, my children, my work, and other good things—have no money-back guarantees. You may have noticed that I said earlier that my time spent has "potential" to reap rewards. That is in contrast to my time committed to the Lord. God's Word carries guarantees: "Ask and it will be given to you; seek and you will find; knock and the door will be opened to you. For everyone who asks receives; he who seeks finds; and to him who knocks, the door will be opened" (Matthew 7:7–8).

Time spent in God's Word and in prayer are seconds, minutes, and hours well spent!

> *[My word] will not return to me empty, but will accomplish what I [God] desire and achieve the purpose for which I sent it. (Isaiah 55:11)*
>
> *The prayer of a righteous man is powerful and effective. (James 5:16)*

TAKING TIME

Even though many of us have an intellectual knowledge that prayer changes things and that God's Word gives life, it can still be difficult to carve out that all-important time. One of the positive aspects of being a home-based-business mom is the beauty of being able to control your schedule to a large degree. You are your own boss. This luxury can definitely aid in the scheduling of your time apart with God. By the same token, however, it is possible that being your own boss just means that you have a driven taskmaster for a boss. Too often, the drive and desire that lead you to choose a home-based business can lead you to rob yourself of time alone with the Lord.

We read in John 10:10, "The thief comes only to steal and kill and destroy; I have come that they may have life, and have it to the full."

I believe that one thing the devil thoroughly enjoys stealing from us is our time of quiet with the Lord. The robbery is committed in broad daylight with the compliance of the victim. We allow ourselves to become distracted and overbooked. We convince ourselves, "Today I am too busy for time apart, but tomorrow I'll get back on task." These excuses are made to assuage any guilt, but more effective than the motivation of guilt is the motivation of love.

ALONE-TOGETHER TIME

My husband, now a pilot in the U.S. Air Force Reserves and a farmer, has had a very busy winter. The unit that he commands is short on pilots, and he has found himself flying many sorties each week. Recently, after three twelve-plus-hour days in a row, he was finally home with me. But we weren't home for long, because Jonathan was scheduled to play in a high school basketball game. We took him to the school very early to prepare for the game, and we went into the gym. Another game was in progress. As former basketball coaches, we both enjoy the game. But right then, there was nothing I wanted more than to have John all to myself—to talk about the events of the last three days.

I asked John if he wouldn't mind sitting in the balcony until Jonathan's game began. In the deserted balcony we were able to talk and laugh and catch up. We were alone—together.

It is God's desire that *our* desire is to have that alone-together time with Him too. Do you want to sneak away to a solitary place where you can have God "all to yourself"? When was the last time you relished the idea of God wanting to share alone time with you? A home-based business, with its flexible schedule and its potentially flexible boss (that's you!) can encourage those precious daily meetings with the Lord. Or, if allowed to, a home-based business can control you and rob you of your meeting time with God.

MARY AND MARTHA

Let's take a look at Mary and Martha. These are two women who apparently set their own hours and schedules and who operated *very* differently.

As Jesus and his disciples were on their way, he came to a village where a woman named Martha opened her home to him. She had a sister called Mary, who sat at the Lord's feet listening to what he said. But Martha was distracted by all the preparations that had to be made. She came to him and asked, "Lord, don't you care that my sister has left me to do the work by myself? Tell her to help me!" "Martha, Martha," the Lord answered, "you are worried and upset about many things, but only one thing is needed. Mary has chosen what is better, and it will not be taken away from her." (Luke 10:38–42)

Both Mary and Martha were fond of Jesus, but they chose to respond to His visit in distinctly different ways. Mary "sat at the Lord's feet listening to what He said," and Martha was "distracted by all the preparations."

I do not want to admit the number of times I have been "distracted by all the preparations" when I could have chosen to give my attention to the Lord and to listen to Him. Choosing, in fact, is the key. "Mary has *chosen* what is better," Jesus said. No one forced Mary to sit at Christ's feet. She chose to do it.

One of the things I love about a home-based business is that I have so many choices and options. No one tells me what time to go to work, what to do at work, or when to stop working. I have choices, just like Mary and Martha did. Sometimes our choices are so prolific that they threaten to strangle us. Do not miss out on the delight of choosing time committed to Christ.

COMMIT YOUR WAYS

A friend recently told several of us some long-range goals he had set on New Year's Eve five years before. He had three items he wished to accomplish by his thirtieth birthday, then some ten years off. He wanted (1) to be married, (2) to be a teacher. and (3) to be a part of a vital ministry. This young man had just married in the fall. He was serving an evangelical church as their pastor, and the day before he had received an invitation to be an adjunct professor at a university near his home.

Tim marveled that every item on his list had been met . . . and he wasn't even thirty yet! I rejoiced in God's grace just as Tim did, and I recalled the verse, "Delight yourself in the LORD and he will give you the desires of your heart" (Psalm 37:4).

Had Tim been able to check off those three goals because he had worked so hard, or because the perfect woman just happened to fall in love with him, or because he was a preacher extraordinaire? No, although he did, she did, and he is. He was able to meet those goals because they were formulated by a man whose heart and ways were committed to the Lord. God gives us the desires of our hearts because, as someone delighting in Him, He puts those desires into our hearts. Mere man-fashioned goals or objectives will not necessarily be achieved. God guarantees the desires of your heart, however, when your life and desires are grounded in your delight of Him. That in itself is motivating to me to spend time seeking, asking, and knocking. Let the flexibility of your home-based business create consistent, quality, committed times with the Lord.

YOUR CHILDREN AS STUDENTS

The same home-based-business flexibility that can provide you with alone-together time with God can allow you to find teachable moments with your children.

Fix these words of mine in your hearts and minds; tie them as symbols on your hands and bind them on your foreheads. Teach them to your children, talking about them when you sit at home and when you walk along the road, when you lie down and when you get up. (Deuteronomy 11:18–19)

As a home-based-business mom, ideally you are there when your children "sit at home . . . walk along the road . . . lie down and . . . get up," and you can use those times to teach God's Word to your children. Those opportunities are examples of quality time in the midst of quantity time. By delighting in my time commitment to God, I am fixing His words in my heart and mind. Those words are there, readily available to discuss with my children. Finding opportunities to talk about God's Word in everyday circumstances is what I like to call experiencing "God moments" or teachable moments.

Teachable moments are not usually scheduled. They don't always occur in the structure of family devotions or in Bible study or Sunday school class. Many times they occur in the dailyness of life, in the quantity time we have with our children.

As a home-based-business mom, I was there to field many of my children's questions and provide them with answers based on God's Word.

"Do some people in heaven have mustaches?" Matthew asked me one day.

Now that is a question for you Bible scholars! Even more intriguing to me than the answer to that question, however, was the motivation he had for asking it. "That's a tough one. I'll need to do a little research to see if I can discover the answer. But tell me, Matthew," I said, "why do you want to know?"

"Well," he explained, "you have a picture of Grandpa Workman [my father] on the shelves behind your desk. And he has a mustache. I never saw Grandpa except in pictures, and I just didn't know if I'd recognize him in heaven if he didn't have his mustache."

I would never have guessed *that* one! I may not have known much about mustaches, but I did know that God's Word says that in heaven we will be able to recognize people. I could tell Matthew that, teaching him what I had learned from God's Word.

This lesson didn't occur during our family devotions or during bedtime prayers. As I recall, he asked me about Grandpa as he sat on the floor of my home office, "working" with his stickers and colors as I worked at my desk. I'm so glad our desks were in the same space. A home-based business gives you opportunities like those. You are there when your children "sit at home . . . walk along the road . . . lie down and . . . get up."

YOUR CHILDREN AS TEACHERS

I remember reading our devotional story one morning and experiencing another teachable moment. Actually this was one in reverse, with Mom doing the learning.

We had just finished reading the story of Peter walking on the water.

During the fourth watch of the night Jesus went out to them, walking on the lake. When the disciples saw him walking on the lake, they were terrified. "It's a ghost," they said, and cried out in fear. But Jesus immediately said to them: "Take courage! It is I. Don't be afraid." "Lord, if it's you," Peter replied, "tell me to come to you on the water." "Come," he said. Then Peter got down out of the boat, walked on the water and came toward Jesus. But when he saw the wind, he was afraid and, beginning to sink, cried out, "Lord, save me!" Immediately Jesus reached out his hand and caught him. "You of little faith," he said, "why did you doubt?" (Matthew 14:25–31)

"Well," began the same child who had questioned me about Grandpa's mustache, "I know why Peter sank."

"You do?" I said in disbelief. "OK, tell me why Peter sank."

"Easy," said Matthew. "He quit lookin' at Jesus!"

Hmmmmmmm . . . I checked the Scripture. "But when he [Peter] saw the wind, he was afraid and, beginning to sink, cried out, 'Lord, save me!'" (v. 30). The boy was right! And how applicable that truth was. When do I sink in my own life? When I look at my circumstances . . . when I see the wind . . . and quit lookin' at Jesus! As a home-based-business mom, teachable moments can abound for your child and for you.

TWENTY-FOUR HOURS

I don't want to suggest that a mom who chooses to work outside the home cannot choose to commit time to be alone with the Lord each day and to find those moments to "sit at home, walk along the road, lie down, and get up" with her children. The difficulty with not being home is in finding adequate time for all the time commitments inside and outside the home. There are only twenty-four hours in a day, and there is no way any of us can change that reality.

I once heard it said that the idea of "time management" was in error. The point was that we cannot manage time. Time will move forward at the same pace day in and day out, and there is not one thing we can do to alter its path. Instead, the suggestion was made that we should strive for *personal* management.

The point is well taken. Nevertheless, let's spend some time taking a good look at the Master Plan, an effective plan of (you guessed it) time management.

PART THREE:

USING YOUR TIME WISELY

"The Master Plan is based in an age-old tenet of time management—routine."

16

ESTABLISHING BALANCE IN YOUR HOME AND BUSINESS:

YOUR TIME MANAGEMENT

I can first remember being aware of time as a precious commodity when I entered college. Up to that point, it seemed that there was always adequate (if not abundant) time to accomplish the tasks of each day. I was an active teenager, but I cannot recall feeling time pressures or imagining that there was not enough time to meet the day's demands. My days were scheduled by school and extracurricular activities that left me with very little time to personally manage.

And then came college. I suddenly had more hours in my day that I was allowed to balance. No longer were the hours of eight to three-thirty dictated by a set schedule of classes. Instead, I had a nine o'clock, an eleven o'clock, and a three o'clock class, and all those hours in between were mine to manage. And managing those hours well was essential to my academic success. I instantly became aware of and interested in time management. How could I best use the "unscheduled" times? How could I meet my class deadlines for reading, writing papers, and preparing for tests in the most effective and efficient manner? How could I manage the hours in my day?

That period of time in my life introduced me to two important and universal components of time management. The first was the fundamental and elementary realization that *every* task takes time. Taking a shower takes time. Eating a meal takes time. Getting dressed takes time. Putting on make-up and doing hair take time. Washing, drying, and folding clothes takes time. Even traveling from one place to another takes time.

BEAM ME UP

I had a good friend in college who never allowed for travel time. When we arranged to meet somewhere at a certain time, I would arrive on time and then calculate his estimated arrival time based on his point of departure. If he left from the art building on the other side of campus, he would be fifteen minutes late. If he had been at the stadium, he would only be five minutes late. I often imagined how long the wait might have been if he had been traveling from his parents' home out of state!

I guess that somewhere in the recesses of his mind was the idea that perhaps this time he would be transported from point A to point B—just like on Star Trek. He would simply command, "Beam me up, Scotty," and would be dematerialized at the departure point and materialized at the final destination. To my knowledge, that hasn't happened yet . . . although I believe my friend is still hopeful (and tardy).

THE BENEFIT OF ROUTINE

Another tenet of time management that became evident to me at this point in my life was the benefit of routine. By establishing a daily morning routine, for example, I was able to accomplish the mundane tasks associated with starting each day in a calculated, predictable, efficient manner. If every morning I began with a shower, breakfast, and then doing my hair and make-up, all those things were likely to be accomplished more efficiently than if I had no routine.

If I routinely parked my bike in the same bike rack outside of the English building, I didn't have to search wildly for it after class was dismissed. If I kept a running list of needed items, I was more likely to purchase all the necessities when I went to the store. Routine saved me time.

PUT IT AWAY

When our sons were twelve, ten, and six years old we moved from a very small home to a much larger one. In the small home, all the boys shared a bedroom. In our larger home every boy had his own room. Each one of the boys managed to spread out and to fill every inch of his new room. My expectations for tidiness were not exceedingly high, and as a result they had no problem meeting my expectations. When our eldest son, Matthew, went to college, he managed to maintain his friendship with his roommate, Brian, but Brian's fondness of Matthew was not based on Matthew's ability to keep his side of the room neat.

Then our next son, Aaron, headed for the university, and I imagined him living in an even bigger mess than his older brother (based on past performance).

But much to my surprise, in the first semester Aaron chose to keep his things put away—something I'm sure his roommate appreciated. The second semester he moved into a single occupancy room and maintained the same high level of neatness he had established during the first semester. It didn't matter whether I arrived on a planned visit or unannounced, his room was always tidy.

Ah, I thought, *he has turned over a new leaf. Neatness and organization have now become a part of his life.*

And then he moved home for the summer, and reality landed with a thud. His room at home was just as messy and cluttered as it had always been. "What's the deal, Aaron?" I asked. "How come you kept your college room immaculate and you're content to have your room at home a junk pit?"

His answer? He informed me that he had no option at school. He didn't have time to look for his room key—so he always put it on the little hook by the door. He couldn't afford to lose his biology notes, so he filed them right after class. His coat took up too much space if it was flung onto his chair, so he always put it away (and knew where it was). All these things became routine, and all the routine saved him time.

17

THE MASTER PLAN
OF TIME MANAGEMENT

In college I began to explore the power of time management. I discovered the importance of honestly evaluating the time required for specific tasks, and I learned the importance of routine. This helped me a great deal as I managed my time. Then I took my first teaching position and again relinquished the majority of the hours of my day to someone else's management. I arrived at school at 7:30 A.M. and departed at 4:00 P.M., and most of the hours spent there were necessarily programmed by the class schedule and the curriculum.

After four years of teaching I discovered that we had a baby on the way, and, when the fall of 1978 arrived, I didn't go to school. It was the first time in twenty-one years! Now no one was dictating the management of my time. Sure I had a baby to care for, and I had household responsibilities, but I was the one in charge of the scheduling of each task and assignment. And I actually had more time than I had amusing assignments. (Key word? Amusing.)

I should clean out the refrigerator today, I would think. *No, I can wait until tomorrow.*

And I suppose I could wait, because I had no specific job set for tomorrow or the next tomorrow. Can you see how my lack of motivation and poor time management might cause a problem? My procrastination and disinterest were a sorry combination. After a year and a half of motherhood, I began my home-based business and had additional responsibilities to put into my schedule. It was then that I stepped back and took note of my downward spiral. I was spending several days in a row in my sloppy bib overalls. I was not accomplishing even minor household chores. And I was very dissatisfied with my disorganization and lack of motivation. I knew that I could not possibly handle a home-based business and a home if I did not get organized. I needed to manage my time more wisely.

"Enough!" I declared, and I recalled my college days, the other time in my life when I was given the opportunity to schedule the majority of the hours in my day. I remembered the importance of establishing routine and of determining the time a task required for completion. Then I set out to become more productive and to adjust my attitude and raise my enjoyment of each day.

THE MASTER PLAN

My new determination gave birth to the Master Plan. I had finally realized that I was allowing time to slip through my fingers—unused and unappreciated. Time is a gift given daily in an equal amount to each and every person. There is no preferential treatment when it comes to the gift of time given each day. And in addition to being equally distributed to all, it is also limited. There are only 60 seconds in a minute—only 60 minutes in an hour—only 24 hours in a day—and only 365 days in a year. You cannot borrow time. You can't eliminate a portion of time from your day, and you can't stretch an hour in a day. Time is a resource that is distributed equally and in finite amounts to all. There's no changing that. All we can hope to do is to manage ourselves within those days, hours, minutes, and seconds, and use the gift of time.

The Master Plan is based on an age-old tenet of time management —routine—and it is especially useful for the home-based-business mom who is walking the tightrope to her goals of loving and serving the Lord, caring for her family, and managing a home-based business. As with any tightrope walker, balance is fundamental! And the routine of the Master Plan can help a home-based-business mom stay in balance.

THREE EASY STEPS

Years ago, my brother-in-law bought a small above-ground pool for his children. He asked my husband, John, if he would be able to help him with the assembly, and he explained that the box said that it was a matter of three easy steps. John agreed to help, and early one Saturday morning they began to tackle the pool construction.

Step 1—Remove sod. Wow! This step was a little more involved than they had anticipated. In fact removing the sod from the area took almost half the morning.

Step 2—Level ground. This step required the use of a transit and a whole lot more shoveling. As I recall, lunch was a midway break in Step 2.

Step 3—Assemble pool. By the time they got to this "final easy step," my niece had changed into her shorts. (She had expectantly started the day in her swimming suit.) The men were a little less optimistic about ever completing the project, and the pool's manufacturer (with his "three easy step" marketing plan) was no longer held in high esteem.

These sweet men did finish assembling the pool, but not before the sun set on Saturday. With this story as background, I reluctantly tell you that the Master Plan has . . . three easy steps.

Just like the construction of the children's pool, these steps will take time and effort. I feel certain, however, that your benefits will far exceed your effort.

Step 1: List Your Commitments

The first step in using the Master Plan is to make a list of your commitments—everything you do on a daily basis (Monday–Friday). *Everything?* Well, everything that takes time. (Which, by the way, is everything.) Where should you begin? How about writing down "get up." I would imagine that each one of you does that particular task on a daily basis. What other things do you do each day? If you are the cook at your home, you probably cook at least once a day. Do you exercise daily? Do you wash your hair each day? Many of you probably wash the dishes each day, maybe even two times each day. How about straightening the house, or making home-based-business calls, or putting on make-up? Do you spend some time each day reading the Bible and praying? Do you pack lunches for your children? Do you read to them each day? Do you drive your children to school? The possible entries on the list are endless!

Hopefully the questions I have asked have begun to prime the pump of your thinking. Try to remember everything that you do on a daily basis. This may be difficult for you, and you might even have to live through a day or a week with the Master Plan in mind before you can make note of all the things you do each day. Get an inexpensive notebook and jot down each task until you have compiled a list that is fairly complete. You can use headings like those on the sample sheet on page 137 [Master Plan Step 1].

Now list your weekly tasks. List all the things you do once or twice a week. Do you wash clothes once a week? Do you drive your children to lessons of any sort once or twice a week? How about cleaning, grocery shopping, or correspondence? You probably spend time each week at church or at a Bible study. Here's where you note the things you may do on Saturday or Sunday differently than on the other days.

There are also activities and time commitments that occur once each month. Do you have business meetings once a month? Do you have civic or church commitments that happen only once a month? Do you have responsibilities as a mom or a wife that occur only once or twice a month?

THE MASTER PLAN

STEP 1

List Your Commitments

TIME MANAGEMENT SYSTEM

DAILY (M–F)

WEEKLY

MONTHLY/BI-MONTHLY

*"Locked-in" times—begin with these

It is important that you write down everything that you do on a regular basis *if* it takes time . . . and most things do. Most things take time even if we are unwilling to recognize that fact or to allow the logical amount of time for their completion. If you do something, write it down in the daily, weekly, or monthly columns. If you would like to view a sample list, you can refer to the example of step 1 on page 139 [Master Plan Step 1 completed]. This is a page I completed years ago. I could give many different examples of step 1 that I have done through the years because my lists of commitments have not remained the same. The one unchanging aspect of motherhood is that change will occur . . . often. Different ages and stages bring different commitments. One of the useful aspects of the Master Plan is its flexibility. As your life changes, your time management plan is easily adapted.

The last requirement of step 1 involves marking each item on your lists that has a predetermined time when it must occur—a locked-in time. Put a star by these things. These are items that must occur at a specific, relatively unchanging time each day. For example, if one of the commitments listed in step 1 is to see that your child is off to school each day on the 7:30 A.M. bus, that is a locked-in time. The school has predetermined the bus's route and time of arrival. If choir is on Wednesday evening at 7:00 P.M., that is a locked-in time. After you have marked all the locked-in times, you are ready to begin step 2.

Step 2: Plug In Daily Tasks

Step 2 involves inserting the daily (Monday–Friday) items into a "skeleton day." (See page 140 [Master Plan Step 2] for an illustration.) The day is divided into morning, afternoon, and evening. Begin with the daily locked-in items you starred in step 1. These times have been established as nonnegotiable (at least for the present time). We will work from these points.

After you have inserted all the locked-in daily times, you are ready to determine the most efficient, effective placement of the other daily commitments you have listed in step 1. Return to the example of

THE MASTER PLAN

STEP 1

List Your Commitments

TIME MANAGEMENT SYSTEM

DAILY (M–F)

get up ☺
cook—3 times
dishes—2 times
prayer and quiet time
family devotions
time with John
shower or bath
make-up
lay out kids' clothes
straighten house
*bus departure 7:30 A.M.
*bus arrival 4:00 P.M.
*business call 7:35 A.M.
*kids to bed 8:00 P.M.

WEEKLY

*choir—Wed. 7:00 P.M.
*Bible study—Tues. 7:00 P.M.
groceries
errands
cook—big batches
correspondence
nap
hair—2 times
exercise—3 times
*drive to band—Wed. 7:10 A.M.
*Sunday school—Sun. 9:00 A.M.
*church—Sun. 10:15 A.M.
family night
*swim lessons—Wed. 1:30 P.M.
*piano lesson—Tues. 4:00 P.M.
wash—2 times
clean
business letters & bookkeeping—2 times
book shows—2 times

MONTHLY/BI-MONTHLY

*youth group—2nd and 4th Sun. 6:00 P.M.
*church board—1st Sunday 5:00 P.M.
*U.T.A. (reserves) weekend—3rd weekend
*sales meeting—2nd Sat. 9:00 A.M.
change sheets—2 times
clean refrigerator—2 times

* "Locked-in" times—begin with these

THE MASTER PLAN

STEP 2

Plug In Daily (M–F) Tasks

TIME MANAGEMENT SYSTEM

Reasonable and Responsible Times

Noon _____

6:00 _____

* *"Locked-in" times—begin with these*

THE MASTER PLAN

STEP 2

Plug In Daily (M-F) Tasks

TIME MANAGEMENT SYSTEM

Reasonable and Responsible Times

5:30 alarm—shower and make-up (if full day)

6:00 prayer and quiet time

6:30 boys up and straighten

6:45 cook breakfast

7:00 eat—family devotions

*7:30 bus

*7:35 business calls

BLOCK OF TIME 8:00–11:45

11:45 make lunch

Noon lunch and dishes

BLOCK OF TIME 1:00–4:00

*4:00 bus

4:30 cook dinner

6:00 dinner and dishes

　　　　straighten

BLOCK OF TIME 7:00–8:00

*8:00 kids go to bed

　　　　lay out kids' clothes

　　　　time with John

* "Locked-in" times—begin with these

the 7:30 A.M. school bus and assume that is the first locked-in time on your Monday through Friday schedule. (Take note: I did not say that is the first thing you do each day; I said that the bus was the first unchanging time commitment.) To have your child cheerfully ready for the 7:30 bus, he probably will have to have eaten a good breakfast served by 7:00 A.M. If this involves any preparation at all, the cook will have to begin by 6:45. When I am the cook, I do not enjoy being rushed and prefer to be up and dressed before I cook or wake up the children. Working backward from the locked-in bus time of 7:30, I can determine how early I must start my day. That starting time is not actually locked in, but it is determined by the non-negotiable bus time.

You may have to guess or actually time yourself while involved in the tasks on your list. How much time do things really require? Once you have made that determination, try to schedule the flexible daily tasks on either side of the locked-in times but close to them. This will allow for blocks of unused time that can be used for your business tasks or other weekly priorities. These blocks of time will materialize on your step 2 schedule if you effectively organize your daily commitments. Although time fragments are valuable, you will accomplish more in a block of time than in ten- or fifteen-minute segments. There is a sample of a completed step 2 for your reference on page 141 [Master Plan Step 2 completed].

Step 3: Plug In Weekly, Monthly, and Bi-Monthly Tasks

Now you are ready for step 3. This step involves the scheduling of weekly tasks into your blocks of time. There is a sample of an uncompleted step 3 skeleton schedule on page 143 [Master Plan Step 3]. The days of the week are indicated across the top of this skeleton schedule. Go back to step 1 and check your weekly items that have locked-in times. Put these items on step 3. The blocks of time that you discovered in step 2 will provide the necessary time allotments for the remainder of the weekly commitments. What weekly items do you want to insert on Monday? Tuesday? Wednesday? At this point you determine how you will schedule your blocks of time

THE MASTER PLAN

STEP 3

Plug In Weekly, Monthly, and Bi-Monthly Tasks

TIME MANAGEMENT SYSTEM

Look for Blocks of Time

MON	TUE	WED	THU	FRI	SAT	SUN

Noon _____

6:00 _____

* "Locked-in" times—begin with these

THE MASTER PLAN

STEP 3

Plug In Weekly, Monthly, and Bi-Monthly Tasks

TIME MANAGEMENT SYSTEM
Look for Blocks of Time

MON	TUE	WED	THU	FRI	SAT	SUN
		*7:10 drive to band	exercise hair	exercise (change sheets)	exercise	hair

BLOCK OF TIME 8:00–11:45

MON	TUE	WED	THU	FRI	SAT	SUN
book show	book show	business letters & book-keeping, etc. wash	business cont.	wash cook– big batches	clean *2nd sales meeting	*Sunday school *church

Noon _____

BLOCK OF TIME 1:00–4:00

MON	TUE	WED	THU	FRI	SAT	SUN
book show	book show *4:00 piano	*1:30 swim lessons errands & groceries	business, cont.	wash cook		nap correspon-dence

6:00 _____

BLOCK OF TIME 7:00–8:00

MON	TUE	WED	THU	FRI	SAT	SUN
*7:00 Bible study	*7:00 choir			"Family Night"	*3rd U.T.A. weekend *1st Sun-Board *2nd & 4th Youth	

( ) Every other week
* *"Locked-in" times—begin with these*

over the course of a week. On page 144 [Master Plan Step 3 completed], a sample step 3 has been finished. This may help you as you complete this step.

FREQUENTLY ASKED QUESTIONS, OR "WILL IT WORK?"

QUESTION: On the step 2 schedule of daily commitments, you indicate that you get up at 5:30 Monday through Friday. I don't want to get up at 5:30 in the morning. Do I have to?

ANSWER: No! You can get up whenever you want, but if your child leaves on the bus at 7:30, you had better at least get up at 7:29 so that you can yell good-bye to him on his way out the door, or smooch him, or whatever you do.

One little tip that I can tell you is something I learned several years ago. I always used to say that I had a problem getting up. Then one day it dawned on me that I had a problem going to bed. You know, it's 9:30 P.M. and the creative juices start flowing. Everyone is quiet . . . your hubby's reading and the children are snoring. You start to think about the managers' meeting coming up next week. You start scribbling notes, and before long your husband asks you if you are ready to go to bed. "Sure, honey. I'll be there in just a minute." He goes to bed and you keep working. More than a minute passes before you finally hit the sack—and lo and behold, it is impossible to get up the next morning. Be aware of your habits and acknowledge and accept them or change them.

QUESTION: If I set reasonable and responsible times, everything that I have said yes to does not fit on my schedule. Is that possible?

ANSWER: Yes! It is very possible that you are overcommitted. The truth of the matter is that God only gives us twenty-four hours a day and we have to use some of it for rest and recuperation. It is important that we make choices as to how we will spend our time. Failing to make deliberate choices is still choosing. Be aware of the choices you are making. Women have a great tendency to become overcommitted. We choose to do good things and sacrifice the better or even the best. Use the Master Plan to help you say no to time robbers and to keep your priorities in order.

QUESTION: What if something special comes up on Monday and I've already scheduled myself for that time?

ANSWER: If your time block is not filled with a "locked-in" item, you can have a great deal of flexibility. If you know ahead of time that this special opportunity is arriving, you can attempt to accomplish your Monday commitments prior to the special event. With the Master Plan, you know what responsibilities you will have to reschedule and you can do them earlier or later if you have an available block of time.

QUESTION: I noticed on the sample sheets that there was actually a nap scheduled! I haven't had time for a nap in years. I'm too busy. How is it possible to actually count on one?

ANSWER: The answer lies in the freeing nature of routine. The Master Plan is based on this principle of time management. If you know that you have scheduled yourself to wash clothes on Monday morning, the full hamper should not bother you during your Sunday afternoon nap. You can rest knowing that the task will be accomplished on schedule the next day.

QUESTION: There are some things that I don't want to reschedule —like my morning shower or my devotional time. Where should I schedule those to see that they happen each day?

ANSWER: I have found that if you do things early in the morning you are less likely to be disturbed. Very few people will call you before 7:00 A.M., and very few locked-in commitments begin before that time.

QUESTION: My life changes constantly. How can I keep a routine with all these changes?

ANSWER: The Master Plan adapts well to change. All that is necessary is evaluation and rescheduling when you realize that your situation has changed. Mothers with young children need to alter their Master Plan every six months or so. As your children get older, the changes are less frequent.

PUTTING THE MASTER PLAN INTO ACTION, OR "READY-FIRE-AIM"

If the Master Plan is something that excites you at all, I think you need to spend about two or three weeks working with it—shifting things around and evaluating the schedules you have set. Remember, Rome wasn't built in a day. Above-ground swimming pools don't materialize in a matter of moments, and learning to manage your time will not happen overnight either. You might think that it takes you five minutes to take a shower when it actually takes you thirty-five! Many times we don't realize the time that is committed to something. Post your Master Plan steps 2 and 3 in prominent places—on the refrigerator, at your desk, near your bed. At first you may not remember that the block of time you have created on Tuesday is to write or wash clothes or run errands. Having the Master Plan within view might save you from distractions or from starting another task.

A monthly calendar can play a big part in keeping you on task. In the old days when I first began to use the Master Plan, my calendar held all my appointments and speaking engagements, but a day scheduled to wash clothes appeared to be a free day on the calendar. My tendency was to accept invitations and fail to remember what my Master Plan had scheduled for that time slot.

Now I use a very simple color code in my calendar. A yellow highlighter stripe through the morning time (top $\frac{1}{3}$ of the day) indicates to me that I have household responsibilities. Yellow represents sparkling clean in my code. Green denotes working. Blue indicates time to be spent with my family. For example, when our boys were younger, we were striving to have one night each week at home as a family. I put a blue stripe through the evening time of the day we'd chosen to remind me not to make another commitment for that time. Hot pink represents activities that are typically "other good things,"

number five on my list of priorities (i.e., church, choir, or civic responsibilities).

Having the Master Plan schedule color-coded keeps us from
overcommitting and forgetting about the routine tasks we must accomplish for survival and to help us reach our goals. The colors can
also help us evaluate the categories of our time commitments at a
glance.

EVERY AVAILABLE RESOURCE

I have a friend, William, who has an identical twin. When William
was in college, he enrolled in a speech class. In preparation for their
demonstration speech, the professor encouraged the members of the
class to use "every available resource." William decided to give a
speech on men's fashion, and he recruited his identical twin brother
to help him. In the first part of the speech, William presented the basics of current men's fashion. Then he exited the room, gave his shoes
to his twin brother who was dressed in a different outfit, and the twin
entered to present a small segment of the speech. When he finished,
he exited, and William reentered almost immediately in a third out-
fit and finished the presentation.

The class was fascinated and the teacher applauded an excellent
speech. "It is obvious how William accomplished this interesting
demonstration speech," she declared. "The key was actually in this
speech. It was the layered look!" The professor gave him an A+ that
day. Later she learned that she had not accurately determined the key
to William's clever speech. When the next class was dismissed, she
asked to speak with my friend. "William, I have changed your grade
to an F. I discovered that you did not give your speech alone, but
instead tricked me with the help of your twin!"

Needless to say, William was devastated, but he was not yet de-
feated. "Yes," he replied, "I did have the help of my brother for the
very short middle segment of my speech. But I was only following
your instructions. You told us to use every available resource, and I
just happen to have a twin brother as an available resource. I didn't

mean to deceive you. I thought you'd know right away. When you didn't, I should have told you. I'm sorry."

The professor pondered the situation briefly and then graciously admitted that, indeed, William had followed directions, and she reestablished his grade as an A+. He had used a unique resource available only to him.

Examine your own resources. I had a friend whose husband had a camping ministry. From mid-May through October they had campers on their property and a full-time cook. When the cook was at the camp, my friend's family ate in the mess hall . . . the food prepared by the cook. The first time I heard about the situation I thought, *No wonder this woman is such a success in her home-based business. Why, I could achieve great things too, if I had a cook.* Bologna! (No pun intended.)

Each of us has a multitude of resources, some of which we've probably never even recognized. Don't covet someone else's resources. Discover your own. Take some time to brainstorm about your own unique resources. I have a very supportive and creative husband. He is one of my greatest resources. Discover *your* resources.

MAKING YOUR MASTER PLAN WORK FOR YOU

When my children were younger, they had a Master Plan. Children thrive on routine and sameness. They like to know that each day will begin and end at a similar time with a similar routine. If there is a routine, your children can anticipate their responsibilities and will accept them more readily.

You can also establish a yearly Master Plan, putting things on the calendar for the year. (Wow, this woman is a fanatic!) For example, a yearly Master Plan allows you to anticipate Christmas (December 25 year after year) and to schedule all the fun and activities you don't want to miss. I used to bake Christmas cookies with my kids. We did it on the first weekend in December, and I wrote it on my calendar long before December. If something else came up, no problem, we could always do it the weekend before. I like to send Valentine cards. Do you know what happens to me if I haven't anticipated Valentine's Day with the Master Plan? Invariably February 14 comes and goes without any participation. How about winterizing the car? That's something you can put on your yearly plan. You can also schedule putting up the storm windows, writing your Christmas cards, and the dates for vacation Bible school. What about any annual conventions you attend? Put them on your yearly Master Plan and you'll never be surprised.

WHY USE THE MASTER PLAN? (WHY NOT?)

The positive results of successfully employing the Master Plan are unlimited. Here are a few of my favorites.

- *No guilt!* I can rest. I can work. I can play. And I don't have to think, *Oh, I have a million things to do!* I don't have to think that, because with the Master Plan I have already allotted time for my daily and weekly commitments.
- *Peace of mind and tranquility.* If things are routine and scheduled, there are fewer surprises.
- *Honest time evaluation.* Am I spending time doing the things that are most important to me, or am I constantly responding to the urgent matters?
- *Successful use of my time.* This can increase my success in all endeavors and can facilitate the reaching of my family and home-based-business goals.

I want to be prepared for action and also to be self-controlled (1 Peter 1:13). The Master Plan has empowered me to do both of those things. And it can do the same for you!

18

50 NIFTY TIME MANAGEMENT HINTS

In addition to employing the Master Plan over the years, I have read many articles and books on time management and have gleaned several helpful hints. Below you will discover a list of fifty of those hints that have genuinely helped me as a home-based-business mom. Because our lives as moms change rapidly and we are continually working ourselves out of a job, some of these hints no longer are applicable in my home. But the chance exists that several of them may be precisely what you can use to manage your time more wisely.

1 PLAN YOUR MENUS AHEAD. Typically the ads for the grocery stores arrive at your home on one day each week. That day or the following one might be a good time to determine your menus for the week based on sales and specials at your local store. I have found that it is not efficient to shop at multiple grocery stores to save a few cents. I usually choose the one with the most appealing sales that week.

In order to achieve some balance in my menus, I determined that each day would feature a different category of entrée. For example, the main course would be beef on Monday, chicken on Tuesday, leftovers on Wednesday, pork on Thursday, fish on Friday, vegetarian on Saturday, and out-to-eat on Sunday. Without this routine, I found myself serving one type of entrée almost exclusively.

2 HAVE ROUTINE BREAKFAST MENUS. Raising three children, I discovered that they had different food preferences. (I always wondered if they didn't choose different favorites just to exert their individualism.) In order to satisfy all the different taste preferences and avoid whining and complaining, I established seven unchanging breakfast menus. On Monday we had fried eggs . . . on Tuesday, French toast . . . Wednesday was hot cereal . . . Thursday, scrambled eggs . . . Friday, pancakes . . . Saturday, cereal . . . and Sunday, sweet rolls or coffee cake. The comment, "Mom, I don't like eggs," was combated with the answer, "No problem. We won't have them tomorrow."

3 COOK IN LARGE BATCHES AND FREEZE. It takes a certain amount of time to make a pan of lasagna. It does not take three times that amount of time to make three pans of lasagna.

4 SHOP FOR GROCERIES ONCE A WEEK. This is a way to save time and money. You could even consider shopping online. The small convenience fee might be equal to or even less than the money you spend on impulse items.

5 HAVE AN ONGOING LIST FOR GROCERIES. Put a magnetic pad of paper on your refrigerator and list items you will need to buy on your next trip to the store. When you use the last of the vanilla, put it on the list. Then when you're ready to go to the store, just grab this list.

6 LAY OUT THE CLOTHES YOU (AND YOUR CHILDREN) WILL WEAR. When your children are young, you can save a great deal of stress and confusion by determining the outfits that will be worn to school or to church and putting those outfits out the night before. Then you can see if anything needs repair, washing, or ironing. This is handy for you too!

7 START THE LAUNDRY THE NIGHT BEFORE. When you put a load into the washer (and maybe even into the dryer) before you go to bed at night, it is like having helpers working for you while you sleep. You have a head start on the next day's tasks.

8 BUY DIFFERENT COLORED WASH BASKETS AND HANGERS FOR EACH FAMILY MEMBER. This is a great help to the children as they put their laundry away. Every child knows which basket and which hang-up clothes belong to him.

9 PURCHASE DIFFERENT COLORED TOWELS FOR EACH FAMILY MEMBER. This will cut down on your laundry as each family member is responsible for hanging up his or her own towel.

10 PROVIDE PLENTY OF TOWEL RACKS. If you want everyone to hang up their towels, make it convenient.

11 BUY TOOTHBRUSHES FOR BOTH THE UPSTAIRS AND DOWN-STAIRS BATHROOMS. If you have multiple children and multiple bathrooms, this is a big help. Again, everyone gets his own color (matching their wash baskets, hangers, and towels if possible).

12 HAVE A LONG PHONE CORD OR A PORTABLE PHONE. This can save you a great deal of time. You can chat while you cook or as you are moving from place to place. Be sure not to occupy your mind with something else, however, when you have a business call. You will want to give it your full attention.

13 USE AN ANSWERING MACHINE TO SCREEN YOUR CALLS. As difficult as it may be to hear the phone ring and resist answering it, you will save time as you return the calls at your convenience.

14 AVOID DUPLICATIONS. When you weed the flower bed, for example, put the refuse into a garbage bag right away. Don't put it on the ground and then into a bag.

15 TOSS IT! If you get something in the mail that is of no interest to you, don't put it aside and be forced to handle it again. Toss it in the wastebasket right away.

16 PLACE A WASTEBASKET IN EACH ROOM. This will facilitate "tossing it" and not duplicating your efforts.

17 FILE IT! If you have paperwork that is important to you, don't take the risk of losing it. File it right away.

18 USE TIME FRAGMENTS. Carry a good book or a few note cards in your purse so that if you find yourself waiting in the doctor's office or in the airline terminal, you can use that time wisely.

19 TAKE TIME TO DE-JUNK YOUR PURSE OR BRIEFCASE PERIODICALLY.

20 CHOOSE A LOW-MAINTENANCE HAIRDO.

21 SCHEDULE YOUR NEXT HAIRCUT WHEN YOU LEAVE YOUR LAST.

22 CONSOLIDATE TRIPS FOR ERRANDS. Sometimes you can tag

these trips onto previously scheduled trips. Sometimes it is best to allow one time block for errands weekly or bi-weekly.

23 BEGIN YOUR ERRANDS WITH THE LOCATION FARTHEST FROM HOME. Actually take the time to plan your route. Make sure you don't waste time backtracking. Start at the farthest location and work your way home.

24 ANTICIPATE WHAT IS COMING. Look ahead *and* plan ahead on your calendar. Don't be surprised by Christmas.

25 ELIMINATE WHENEVER POSSIBLE. Do you really have to drive to the bank? Perhaps a call will achieve the same purpose.

26 DELEGATE RESPONSIBILITIES TO OTHERS. There may be a high school girl in your church who could help you with dinner preparation or even with filing or running errands.

27 INSPECT, DON'T EXPECT. When you delegate jobs, be sure to see that they are done as you requested. This is especially important with children.

28 DON'T EXPECT PERFECTION. As you inspect, be an encourager. When you expect perfection from yourself or others, you are bound to be disappointed.

29 USE EVERY AVAILABLE RESOURCE. Remember William the twin.

30 TAKE TIME OUT TO PRAY! Never be foolish and forfeit your time of communication with the Lord. Taking time to pray saves time!

31 TAKE TIME OUT FOR YOUR HUSBAND. This time can take many forms ... conferences, retreats for planning, or romantic times together. Always remember you want to "wear the same color jersey" as your husband, so keep him as a high priority.

62 SCHEDULE A S.A.M.S. Think about establishing a **S**unday **A. M. S**ummit for discussion time with your husband. You probably won't be interrupted before Sunday school time when the kids are still asleep, and you can discuss calendars and plans and/or issues that may have occurred in the previous week. Sunday afternoon may be a better time for you. The time is not as important as the commitment to a weekly summit.

63 TAKE "TIME OUTS" TO REORGANIZE AND REJUVENATE. These can be as simple as a cup of tea in the family room or as involved as a week-long retreat. For me, a few minutes to evaluate how the day's plans are going can be very helpful.

64 MAKE A "TO DO" LIST. Jotting down what you want to accomplish in a day, a week, or even longer will act to keep you on task.

65 PRIORITIZE YOUR "TO DO" LIST. This is a matter of accomplishing first things first. If you have an important call to make before eight, don't start putting clothes in the washer at 7:57.

66 READY, FIRE, AIM! Don't wait for everything to be in order before you begin. You may have to wait forever. You cannot steer a boat tied to the dock. It must be launched. God will be able to steer you as you launch out too.

67 KNOW YOURSELF. I am a morning person. It is best for me to do creative, productive things in the morning. After 4:00 P.M., it is better for me to accomplish "non-thinking" tasks.

68 PURCHASE BIRTHDAY AND OTHER CARDS AHEAD. Shopping for greeting cards can be very time-consuming. When you are buying your brother's birthday card, why not pick up your brother-in-law's? Buying get well and sympathy cards ahead is also helpful. I have a good friend who always buys belated birthday cards ahead. She is a woman who knows herself.

39 HAVE A PERPETUAL BIRTHDAY CALENDAR. This way you might be able to avoid sending a belated card. And you'll remember the important days.

40 ESTABLISH A MASTER CALENDAR AND KEEP IT UP-TO-DATE. I think it is best to make that calendar a portable one that you can have with you in your purse. We also have a big desk calendar that I try to keep current, but the portable one is the "left side of my brain." (That's the organized side!)

41 WRITE IT DOWN. By writing down important (or even not-so-important) information in your calendar, it is readily available. This frees you to think about more important things, like prayer requests. (Which, by the way, I also jot down in a section of my calendar so that I do not forget them.)

42 KEEP A SEPARATE BRIEFCASE OR PORTFOLIO FOR THE DIFFERENT JOBS YOU HAVE. I have several responsibilities at my church. Because of that, I keep one briefcase just for church. I can stuff things into it through the week. When Sunday rolls around, I remove my calendar and my wallet from my everyday briefcase and put them into my church one. Then nothing is forgotten.

43 HAVE A MONEY JAR IN THE KITCHEN. This can hold lunch money and can be available when your wallet may be empty.

44 IF YOU TRAVEL, KEEP A SUITCASE PACKED WITH ESSENTIALS. This is a great way to assure that you will always have your own toothbrush or lipstick.

45 PREPARE A PACKING LIST FOR THE OTHER THINGS. I have a list of items I use consistently at home and that I do not want to buy a duplicate of for my suitcase (i.e., my curling iron and my tennis shoes). I also make a list of current items needed for the particular trip I'm taking—specific outfits, a swimsuit, etc.—and check them off as they are packed.

46 ESTABLISH A ROUTINE FOR THE PLACEMENT OF EVERYDAY ITEMS. Always put your keys in the same place. Keep your glasses and sunglasses in a consistent location. Always return your credit card to its predetermined location. This routine will save you time.

47 PURCHASE ITEMS BY CATALOG AND THE INTERNET. This can be a tremendous time-saver. Usually when you order by phone, the operator will tell you immediately if the item is available. Wandering around a store can be very tiring. (Unless, of course, it is "retail therapy.") It is important for you to know yourself when it comes to this time-saver. If you have been known to waste time poring over a catalog, you might want to avoid this temptation. You also need to be aware of the fact that, after a catalog order, you will receive a vast number of catalogs from other companies. Feel free to throw them away upon arrival.

48 PURCHASE EVERYTHING YOU NEED TO COMPLETE AN OUT-FIT. A beautiful new skirt will never be worn if you don't have a blouse to go with it.

49 TAKE TIME TO TELL YOUR CHILDREN THE DAY'S AGENDA. This will help them be prepared and let them know that you are prepared. When things have to change, they will also learn to be flexible as they see you doing this.

50 "A PLACE FOR EVERYTHING AND EVERYTHING IN ITS PLACE." My mom said it. Your mom said it. And you have probably said it too. When we establish a specific spot for an item and consistently return it to that spot, we save valuable time. In my kitchen cabinets, I have little labels on the shelves ... bread pans, 9x12 pans, round pans, etc. Why? On the outside chance that someone else puts a pan away, he will be able to put it in the right place.

And finally and most importantly, know that each day can be a thing of enjoyment. Never allow your schedule to stifle the plans God has for you. Be ready for opportunities and appointments He provides that may not be in your Daytimer.

19

RECIPES THAT ARE
REALLY EASY . . .
BUT MAKE YOU
LOOK GOOD!

I have tried these recipes and they definitely fit the criteria! Happy cooking and happy eating, Mom! (Each of the cooks named has graciously given me permission to use her recipe.)

GERMAN PANCAKES
6 eggs
1 cup milk
1 cup flour
dash of salt
$\frac{1}{2}$ cup margarine
Mix eggs, milk, flour and a dash of salt. Preheat oven to 400 degrees. Melt the margarine in a 9 x 13 pan in the oven. Pour the mixture into the melted butter. Bake for 25 minutes. Great for a crowd!
Kendra Smiley

BREAKFAST CASSEROLE

1 pound bacon, sausage, or ham	5 eggs
32 oz. Ore-Ida Tater Tots	1 cup milk
8 oz. pkg cheddar cheese	1 can cream of chicken soup
8 oz. pkg mozzarella cheese	

Cook bacon or sausage. Spray 9 x 12 pan with non-stick cooking spray. Put tater tots in pan. Layer meat and cheese. Combine eggs, milk, soup and pour evenly over pan. Bake at 350 degrees for 60 minutes or until eggs are done.

Barb Allen

SOUR CREAM MUFFINS

2 cups biscuit mix
8 oz. sour cream
$\frac{1}{2}$ cup butter, softened

Mix all ingredients together. Drop into greased muffin pan. Bake at 425 degrees for 10 minutes or until golden. Makes 8 muffins.

Cathy Cooper

BUCKET OF MUFFINS

5 cups flour	I quart buttermilk
3 cups sugar	4 eggs
15 oz. box of raisin bran	I cup oil
5 teaspoons baking soda	2 teaspoons salt

Mix all ingredients in a very large bowl. You may keep dough in the refrigerator and use as desired. Bake in muffin cups at 375–400 degrees for 10–12 minutes. Makes more than 4 dozen muffins. They freeze well, also.

Kendra Smiley

ITALIAN BEEF

$\frac{1}{2}$ teaspoon crushed red pepper	I teaspoon onion salt
2 teaspoons basil	4–7 lbs. lean meat
2 teaspoons oregano	(a chuck roast is good)
2 bay leaves	$\frac{1}{2}$ teaspoon black pepper
$\frac{1}{2}$ teaspoon garlic salt	3 cups water
2 teaspoons salt	

Combine all of the above ingredients. Cover and bake at 300 degrees for at least 5 hours. Meat should be tender enough to shred into pieces for sandwiches.

Pam Rush

LASAGNA   1 of 2

1 pound ground chuck	3 eggs
16 oz. package of lasagna noodles	salt and pepper to taste
28 oz. jar of spaghetti sauce	2 8 oz. bags mozzarella cheese
24 oz. cottage cheese	parmesan cheese

Brown the ground chuck and drain off the grease. Spray a 9 x 12 pan wih cooking spray and line the bottom of the pan with $\frac{1}{3}$ of the noodles (uncooked). Combine the browned chuck and the spaghetti sauce. Put $\frac{1}{3}$ of this sauce mixture over the noodles. Combine the cottage cheese, eggs, and a dash of salt and pepper.

continued

LASAGNA   2 of 2

Put $\frac{1}{3}$ of this mixture over the meat sauce. Top this with $\frac{1}{3}$ of the mozzarella cheese. Start again with a layer of noodles, then sauce, then cottage cheese, then mozzarella. Repeat again. Sprinkle the top with Parmesan cheese. Bake covered for 45 minutes at 350 degrees. Remove the cover and bake 15 minutes more. Let stand for 10 minutes before cutting.

Kendra Smiley

SAUCY PORK CHOPS

$\frac{1}{2}$ cup ketchup

$1\frac{1}{2}$ teaspoons salt

$1\frac{1}{2}$ teaspoons chili powder

I cup water

$\frac{1}{2}$ teaspoon dry mustard

I tablespoon brown sugar

4 pork chops

I lemon (optional)

I onion (optional)

Mix the first 6 ingredients. Spray 9 x 13 pan with cooking spray. Place chops in pan. Cover with sauce and one slice of onion and one slice of lemon. Bake at 325 degrees for 2 hours covered and $\frac{1}{2}$ hour uncovered.

Jean Smiley

PORK SPARERIBS

6–8 pounds pork spareribs

I bottle barbecue sauce

Place ribs in a single layer in large baking pans. Bake uncovered at 350 degrees for 30 minutes. Drain. Turn ribs. Bake 30 minutes longer. Drain again and put ribs in the Crockpot. Cover the spareribs with the BBQ sauce. Cook on low for 6–8 hours. Serves 8.

Kendra Smiley

GRILLED CHICKEN BREASTS

$\frac{1}{4}$ cup oil

$\frac{1}{4}$ cup soy sauce

2 tablespoons ketchup

1 tablespoon vinegar

$\frac{1}{4}$ teaspoon pepper

$\frac{1}{2}$ teaspoon garlic powder

4 skinless, boneless chicken breasts

Put all the ingredients in a zipper-seal plastic bag. Marinate for four or more hours. (The longer, the juicer.) Grill over low heat until the chicken is no longer pink—inside and out. Discard the marinade. (An even easier method is to substitute a bottle of Italian salad dressing for the marinade ingredients.)

Lisa Leigh

SUE'S CHICKEN CASSEROLE

2 cups cooked chicken*

2 cups macaroni, uncooked

1 can cream of mushroom soup

1 can cream of chicken soup

2 cups milk or chicken broth

$\frac{1}{2}$ teaspoon salt

$\frac{1}{2}$ teaspoon pepper

$\frac{1}{2}$ cup Velveeta cheese

Combine all the ingredients except the cheese in a 9 x 12 pan. Mix well. Cut the cheese into chunks and put it on top. Cover and bake at 350 degrees for 1 hour.

*I buy chicken breasts and put them into the Crockpot with a little water on low for 6 hours. Then, after they cool, I remove the skin and the bones and cut the meat into pieces. I freeze the meat in 2 cup amounts.

Sue Samet

EASY TUNA CASSEROLE

7 oz. box macaroni

2 cans tuna in spring water

1 can cream of chicken soup

1 can cream of celery soup

2 cups shredded cheddar cheese

Cook the macaroni as instructed on the box. Drain it. Pour cooked macaroni into an oven-safe casserole dish. Add tuna and soups and mix well. Top with cheese. Cover and microwave on high for 10 minutes or bake in the oven for 20 minutes at 350 degrees.

Merissa Wiseman

BAKED FISH

4–6 fish fillets (orange roughy is good)

Butter or margarine

Lemon juice

Place each fish fillet on a separate sheet of foil. Dot each fillet with butter or margarine and pour 2 tablespoons lemon juice over it. Wrap up the fillet in the foil and bake for 30 minutes at 350 degrees.

Kendra Smiley

REFRIGERATOR MASHED POTATOES

5 lbs. boiled potatoes	1 teaspoon salt
1 cup sour cream	6 tablespoons margarine
$\frac{1}{2}$ teaspoon onion salt	4 oz. shredded cheddar cheese
8 oz. cream cheese	

Mash potatoes and add other ingredients, except cheddar cheese. Beat until fluffy. Take out the amount you want to serve. Bake in a casserole dish, uncovered, 30 minutes at 350 degrees. Sprinkle cheese on top and bake for 5 minutes longer. Stores in refrigerator (unbaked) for up to two weeks.

Pam Rush

PLUPERFECT POTATOES

1 large pkg. frozen hash browns	2 tablespoons chopped onion
1 can cream of celery soup	3 tablespoons green pepper
1 can cream of chicken soup	$\frac{1}{2}$ lb. grated colby cheese
1 cup sour cream	1 teaspoon salt

Thaw potatoes. Combine all ingredients in large bowl; place in greased 9 x 13 pan. Bake at 300 degrees for $1\frac{1}{2}$ hours or until potatoes are done.

Rhoda Greene

SCALLOPED CORN

I onion, finely chopped	I can creamed corn
I stick margarine	I pkg. Jiffy corn muffin mix
2 eggs, beaten	I pint sour cream
I can corn, drained	2 cups shredded cheddar cheese

Sauté onion in margarine. Fold corn into beaten eggs. Add muffin mix. Add onion. Pour into 9 x 12 pan and ice with sour cream. Top with cheese. Bake at 350 degrees for I hour. Sprinkle with paprika if desired.

Sue Samet

BROCCOLI CASSEROLE

2 bags frozen broccoli
I can cream of mushroom soup
8 oz. sour cream
2 8 oz. packages shredded cheddar cheese

Cook the broccoli as directed on the package. Put into a 9 x 12 pan. Mix soup and sour cream together. Spread over the broccoli. Sprinkle cheese on top. Microwave on high until cheese melts, or bake at 350 degrees for 10 minutes.

Dilys Lugena

FRUIT SALAD

30 oz. fruit cocktail (drained)

11 oz. mandarin oranges (drained)

1 can peach pie filling

1 bag whole frozen strawberries

Combine fruit cocktail, oranges, and pie filling in a bowl. Cut up frozen strawberries and add to fruit.

Ginger Campbell

MARY'S WHITE SALAD

1 can sweetened condensed milk   1 cup chopped pecans

8 oz. whipped topping   2 tablespoons lemon juice

1 can chunked pineapple, drained very well

Chill all ingredients. Completely drain the pineapple chunks. Use paper towels to get as much juice out as possible. Combine all the ingredients. Chill thoroughly. If your salad does not set up after approximately two hours, you did not adequately drain the pineapple. It will still taste great. Try harder next time.

Mary Houmes

CHEESECAKE PIE

8 oz. cream cheese	I graham cracker crust
⅓ cup powdered sugar	I can fruit pie filling
8 oz. whipped topping	

Combine the first three ingredients. Mix well. Put into the crust. Top with a can of fruit pie filling. (Blueberry and strawberry are especially good.) Chill for 4 hours or overnight.

Judy Clark

DELICIOUS BUTTER COOKIES

I cup butter, not margarine	I teaspoon baking soda
I cup oil	4 cups flour
I cup sugar	I teaspoon cream of tartar
I teaspoon vanilla	I teaspoon salt
2 eggs	

Combine all the ingredients in the order given. Roll into balls and press flat with a sugared glass. Bake 8–10 minutes at 375 degrees.

Bertha Ehard

A GIFT FROM YOUR KITCHEN
. . . SAND CASTLE BROWNIE MIX

$\frac{1}{3}$ cup chopped nuts

$\frac{1}{2}$ cup semisweet chocolate chips

$\frac{1}{3}$ cup flaked coconut

$\frac{2}{3}$ cup packed brown sugar

$\frac{3}{4}$ cup sugar

$\frac{1}{3}$ cup baking cocoa

1$\frac{1}{2}$ cups all purpose flour

In a one-quart glass container, layer the ingredients in order listed, packing well between each layer. Cover and store in a cool dry place for up to 6 months. Yields 4$\frac{1}{4}$ cups total.

continued

A GIFT FROM YOUR KITCHEN
. . . SAND CASTLE BROWNIE MIX

Attach a gift tag listing the following additional ingredients and instructions:

2 eggs

$\frac{2}{3}$ cup vegetable oil

1 teaspoon vanilla

To prepare brownies: In a bowl, combine eggs, oil, vanilla, and brownie mix. Mix well. Spread into a greased 8-inch-square baking pan. Bake at 350 degrees for 30 minutes or until toothpick inserted in center comes out clean. Cool on a wire rack.

Yield: 2 dozen.

Julie Walder

CONCLUSION:
BACK TO
THE BIG TOP

You are now equipped. You have established and painted your priorities. You have identified your job description and noted the time commitment of your homemaking, housekeeping, and family assignments. You have determined reasonable and responsible times for completing your daily commitments, and you have established blocks of time to complete your weekly and monthly commitments. You have been outfitted not only with the functional and adaptable Master Plan, but you have been provided with helpful hints and delicious, nutritious recipes (which do not require you to be ambitious).

You are equipped! You are ready, and now you must choose to walk the tightrope to your goals. Only you can choose to keep your priorities in order and reach your goals of loving and serving your husband and children, honoring God, and having a successful home-based business. No one can force you to make wise time investments, to honestly evaluate your time commitments, or to choose to manage your time wisely. You are alone on the high wire.

What I can do is encourage you. My experience as a home-based-business mom has been and continues to be incredibly fun and rewarding. I did not say it has been easy or without challenge. Just as the tightrope walker in the Big Top occasionally takes two steps forward and then one step backward, my journey to reach my goals has not necessarily been without setbacks. Many times my husband has caught me as I have almost lost my balance. He has gently reminded me of my priorities or has picked up my slack at a busy time. My children have also reminded me of the importance of first things first and have graciously suggested that it was time for a "real meal." For these stabilizing admonitions, I will be forever grateful.

When the graceful acrobat in the Big Top loses her balance without recovery, she is well aware of her mishap as she falls from the high wire to the safety net below. As a home-based-business mom walking the high wire to her goals, it is possible to lose balance and focus and not be aware of the mishap for several years. It may take that long before the detrimental slip is detected as family relationships, our home-based business, or our relationship with the Lord is negatively affected.

There have been times when I almost slipped off the tightrope and times when I wondered if I could recover my balance. But with help, I did, and I'm here to report that the effort to maintain that balance and walk that high wire to my goals of loving and serving John and Matthew, Aaron, and Jonathan, honoring God, and having a successful home-based business was well worth the effort. Reaching the far stand, reaching the goal, is both possible and pleasing. I want to encourage and applaud you as you walk the high wire in your role as a home-based-business mom!

APPENDIX:
BOOKS ON MY SHELF THAT YOU MIGHT WANT ON YOURS

Gwen Ellis. *101 Ways to Make Money at Home.* Ann Arbor, Mich.: Vine Books, 1996.

Cheri Fuller. *Home Business Happiness.* Lancaster, Pa.: Starburst, 1995.

Barbara Hemphill. *Taming the Paper Tiger.* Washington, D.C.: Kiplinger Books, 1992.

Alan Loy McGinnis. *Confidence: How to Succeed at Being Yourself.* Minneapolis: Augsburg, 1987.

June Hines Moore. *The Etiquette Advantage: Rules for the Business Professional.* Nashville: Broadman and Holman, 1998.

Lindsey O'Connor. *The Christian's Guide to Working from Home.* Eugene, Ore.: Harvest House, 1997.

Donna Partow. *Homemade Business: A Woman's Step-by-Step Guide to Earning Money at Home.* Colorado Springs: Focus on the Family, 1999.

Denis Waitley. *Seeds of Greatness.* New York: Simon and Schuster, 1983.

Stephanie Winston. *Getting Organized.* Boston: Warner Books, 1991.

Moody Press, a ministry of Moody Bible Institute,
is designed for education, evangelization, and edification.
If we may assist you in knowing more about Christ
and the Christian life, please write us without obligation:
Moody Press, c/o MLM, Chicago, Illinois 60610.